PRODUCT DESIGN 3

PRODUCT DESIGN

3

By Joe Dolce,
Jaclynn Fischman,
Associate Editor
and the Editors of
ID Magazine

PBC International, Inc. ■ New York

DISTRIBUTOR TO THE BOOK TRADE IN THE UNITED STATES AND CANADA:
Rizzoli International Publications, Inc.
597 Fifth Avenue
New York, NY 10017

DISTRIBUTOR TO THE ART TRADE IN THE UNITED STATES:
Letraset USA
40 Eisenhower Drive
Paramus, NJ 07653

DISTRIBUTOR TO THE ART TRADE IN CANADA:
Letraset Canada Limited
555 Alden Road
Markham, Ontario L3R 3L5, Canada

DISTRIBUTED THROUGHOUT THE REST OF THE WORLD BY:
Hearst Books International
105 Madison Avenue
New York, NY 10016

PBC INTERNATIONAL, INC.
One School Street
Glen Cove, NY 11542.

Library of Congress Cataloging-in-Publication Data

Dolce, Joe.
          Product design 3.

          Includes Index.
          1. Design, Industrial.   I. Industrial design
(New York, N.Y. : 1983)   II. Title.   III. Title:
Product design three.
TS171.D635   1988   745.2   88-18020
ISBN 0-86636-066-2

Color separation, printing and binding by
Toppan Printing Co. (H.K.) Ltd. Hong Kong
Typesetting by **Jeanne Weinberg Typesetting, Inc.**

PRINTED IN HONG KONG
10 9 8 7 6 5 4 3 2 1

Acknowledgments

Thanks to James Andrade and Cynthia Rogers of Rogers-Tropea Inc; Judith Arango; Jacqueline Blumenthal and Susan Becher of Susan Becher Public Relations; Tom di Palma at D.P. Promozione Alternativea, Inc.; Yoshiko U. Ebihara of Gallery 91; Cleveland Evans, Claire Kendall and William Wright of Design Publications, Inc.; Rick Kaufmann of Art et Industrie; John Mattes of *Golf Magazine*; Cara McCarty and Laura Roberts of the Museum of Modern Art; Susan Rosenthal of *Ski Magazine*; Sherry Williams and Clodaugh of Clodaugh Ross Williams; Patricia Roxbury of Stelton U.S.A. Inc.; Leta K.

Stathacos of Artobjects Unlimited; Grant Stit; Akira Takayavu of the Japan Industrial Design Promotion Organization; Terry Temple of *Waterski Magazine*; and Carol Walton of SEE, Ltd.

Special heartfelt thanks to Alexander Polakov, who generously gave his time and valued opinions; Stacy Lucas for tirelessly pitching in; Donna Green for her winning smile and trusted advice; Chee Pearlman for her unflinching support and thoughtful judgment; Annetta Hanna for suggesting I take on this project to begin with, and for

guiding me through those late, late nights; Randolph McAusland for taking a chance on me in the first place and then pushing me to take chances; and Kevin Clark for sticking by.

Finally, this book would not have appeared without the tireless work and energy of Jaclynn Fischman, who never showed even the slightest frustration in her most taxing duties as associate editor. Her exhaustive research and devotion to this project were invaluable and reached well beyond the call of duty.

STAFF

MANAGING DIRECTOR	*Penny Sibal-Samonte*
CREATIVE DIRECTOR	*Richard Liu*
FINANCIAL DIRECTOR	*Pamela McCormick*
ASSOCIATE ART DIRECTOR	*Daniel Kouw*
EDITORIAL MANAGER	*Kevin Clark*
ARTISTS	*Kim McCormick*
	Andy Bork

CONTENTS

INTRODUCTION

Two memorable events initiated my love affair with things. The first occurred when I was a kid and my father took us to eat in a Chinese restaurant. Thanks to the help of a friendly waiter, I learned how to manipulate chopsticks. And though I couldn't articulate the pleasure they brought me at the time, something inside of me was tickled. Eating with chopsticks was almost as much fun as eating with my hands. The slender, polished enamel sticks were like extensions of my fingers, yet they were graceful, rhythmic, exotic. They were the most simply crafted and at the same time most complex tools imaginable.

The second event was when I heard the word "ergonomics." Upon discovering that things were actually made to fit the quirky ways human beings operated, I became aware of the benevolence of science. Until then, I suppose I had presumed that objects were randomly configured, that they somehow just spontaneously came together. Knowing that there were people who actually questioned where to put the handles on doors so that they could be more easily opened, who devised chairs that reduced the strain on our tired backs, who devoted their energies to creating products that enrich the lives of the handicapped, reassured me that there was still a bit of magic and warmth out there in the cold, foreign world of technology.

Since then I have found myself delighted by other objects that are as simple to use as chopsticks and as techno-logically humane as ergonomic seating or wheelchairs. To some extent, we have engineers to thank. But today, more than ever in the past, we must also credit designers. Not only do they act as the translators between technology and human beings, imparting to the nuts, bolts and chips that elusive quality called "personality," but they also build the bridges between the present and the future.

In fact, the 1980s might be called the decade of the designer. In the past few years, awareness of the field has soared as witnessed by the attention, both frivolous and sober, museums, newspapers, popular magazines, television, even motion pictures have given it.

This increased notice is the result of a number of inter-connected factors. Full-swing into the computer age, we find ourselves struggling with yet another phase of the technical revolution that is re-redefining the way we work, play, eat, think,

"Progess" is still moving at breakneck speed—and at times it stands to leave us stunned with confusion. Consider: Just 20 years ago it would have been unimaginable that phones could remember the last number dialed, or that machines would dispense cash 24 hours a day, or that mini-home computers would check the spelling of our children's term papers. Enter the designer, who can make these potentially scary changes understandable, accessible—fun.

"We lead a life of total communication, and design is a way of communicating oneself to others," says Ettore Sottsass, the father of modern Italian design. "The possibility of creating an environment through products or objects is an idea that in ancient times, only kings had. Now almost everybody shares it because there has been this

democratization through design."

While Sottsass' optimistic explanation is correct, it isn't the whole truth. In fact, design awareness has also been spurred by some savvy marketers who have elevated the designer into a star, and consequently sold his or her name to consumers who are wealthy enough, educated enough, status-conscious enough to seek out expensive signatures. Combine that salesmanship with a bland political climate and a modest economic upsurge, and the result is ever more money, time and freedom to devote to the pursuit of polished tastes. Consumerism might well be called the art of our age, and the increased focus on signature wares figures prominently in the aesthetic escapism so rampant today.

At the same time, for the design profession, all this

attention happily translates into better resources, more responsibility and new approaches to old problems. Some of the resulting designs are good and important. Others are inconsequential. In any case, a plethora of objects abounds, both good and bad. It is under these conditions that books like *Product Design 3*, which highlight the best solutions from around the world, become increasingly relevant. And for future evaluation, such books provide an historical context, a platform from which we can survey contemporary design's recent history.

This volume, unlike its predecessors, also attempts to give some insight into the designing mind. Rather than sling our opinions about the future of lighting or vacuum cleaners, we spoke informally with leading designers about what they do

and how they make their decisions. We weren't disappointed with what they revealed.

For one, though originally we had asked each designer to discuss a specific category, more often than not that proved impossible. As designer Andree Putman explains, "For me there is no difference between designing tabletop objects or textiles...It all comes from the same place, the same vision." That sentiment was echoed throughout our conversations. Again and again, we were reminded that design is not a rote technical practice to be perfunctorily applied. Instead, as in film, literature, theatre—any art—it is the idiosyncratic, individual stamp that most often makes the difference between a good product and a great one.

These professionals also agreed that their inspiration, like

the writer's or painter's, arises from a mysterious, undefinable inner-world. "When I design, I try to find truth and beauty for this particular time in history, in this particular culture," says medical designer Gianfranco Zaccai of Design Continuum. "My influences come from all over. I can't cite one simple point of reference and if I could, there would be no art, no mystery in design. It would simply be the application of stylistic gimmicks."

Far-ranging in its scope, *Product Design 3* demonstrates that the art of design encompasses much more than computer terminals or teapots. While any enlightened design should resolve aesthetic questions, it should also extend the function of an object beyond what we currently know, to give consumers enhanced value. Good design or, as Lorenzo Porcelli prefers, "substantial" design, allows an object to speak to us in a new vocabulary, and places that object in an historical stream. It enables a bicycle to say "ride me," a computer to say "type on me," and a chair to say "sit on me."

Rather than labelling trends of the late 1980s, *Product Design 3* surveys the diversity of our designed environment to offer insight into this exciting field. This volume makes clear that virtually every aspect of our lives is being touched by design. In the kitchen or the living room, on the sports field or at the desk, in the factory or in the hospital, the way products look and function is becoming ever more relevant. The challenge of the future will be to equip those in the developing world with some of our tools, and more importantly, to help them devise solutions for themselves.

At a time when the relationship between craft, art, mass production and technology is more convoluted than ever, this book shows the many points of their intersection. And if you closely examine the most complicated machine pictured here, perhaps you'll discover the uncomplicated, childlike inspiration from which it was born. In any case, by the time you've surveyed the products within, you should clearly see the way today's designs reflect the past and portend the future.
                                        —*Joe Dolce*

V. Lorenzo Porcelli
Porcelli Associates

The most important thing I've learned about being a designer came over a lunch I had with the late George Finley, who was the editor of *ID Magazine* in the early '80s. He said that the best designers were also the best editors. I thought about it and discovered that the man was absolutely right. An editor has to know what's important, what to include and what to leave out, how to put things together. And that's what a designer does—visual and sensual editing. Visual because objects are compositional, three-dimensional, and sensual because they have a surface. And if you are a really good designer, you go through the process, see new things, and pick them out.

I don't think it's magic, and I don't think it's mystical. Look at the Italian designers. They go after design with a spirit of nothing to lose and everything to gain. It's the vitality that they bring to projects that allows them to explore wonderful new things.

•

There are two ways to make a product talk to you. One is by understanding its functional aspect, knowing how it works. The second is by exploring the very elusive issue of appeal. Why are some things appealing? Because they have a sensual or a visual quality that is disarming or delightful. And that's the designer's role: to uncover something that hasn't been uncovered before.

Design also works when an object's animation and language is clear and understandable. These qualities are the linguistics of design. But a well-designed product also has to do more work than its predecessors. If it doesn't, we don't need a new chair, kettle or hand pump. These products have been so overdone, we could have a moratorium on them and nobody would suffer. The only reason to do anything new is to make some substantive contribution to the state of the art. Of course I can't always be true to what I just said....

We started out with the water kettle (p. 189) by saying that the

world doesn't need another kettle. Period. The only reason to do another was to articulate our own point of view. And the key word there is "articulate." Just as there is an articulation in language, so is there an articulation in design.

•

Why are architects tackling tabletop these days? Why shouldn't they? First of all, they got a big push from Alessi, which had the great marketing idea of working with big name architects. Tabletop products are a natural because they are such ordinary things, and I don't mean that as a putdown. Ordinary comes from the Latin, "ordinarius," to put in order. And think about it: if you use something every day, then you can't do without it. So maybe these tabletop things are so ordinary—meaning important— that everybody, including architects, has thought about them.

Another thing—in 2,000 years food hasn't changed, the way you serve it hasn't changed, the way you season it hasn't changed, the proportions haven't changed, and the way you sit around the table hasn't changed. Nothing has changed, except for TV dinners. So maybe everyone feels that it is fair game and that they should take a crack at it.

•

Recently, I gave a talk where someone used the expression "good design" and I said, "No one has used that expression for 15 years. It's very outdated and had its place in history in the '50s and '60s." The word I suggested instead was "substance." Design has to be substantive, just like a person. A substantial person is someone who makes you think differently, or at the very least, provokes you into thinking. It's the same with design.

The graphic designer Milton Glaser once said that "there is a degree of innocent vision in design," and I also think the question comes down to that. If you can take this innocence with you, whatever your project, and forget the burdens of the past and all the things that you have seen before, you can bring a new

vision to it. You can get something substantive.

•

One "substantial" person who taught me the most about the magic of metaphor— which has everything to do with design—was Dylan Thomas, the Welsh poet who died much too young at 39. He wrote "A Child's Christmas in Wales," which my family and I listen to every Christmas Eve after midnight Mass. We've been doing this now for 15 years and every time I hear it, I hear something new. And that is the mark of a true work of art: each time it should give you something new and always appear alive. It should never get outdated. It's an incredible lesson because Dylan Thomas had nothing to do with design and yet everything to do with it.

PRODUCT:
Tea Service
DESIGNER
V. Lorenzo Porcelli
MANUFACTURER
Dansk International Designs Ltd.

PRODUCT
''Shato'' Barware and Liquid
Pitchers
DESIGNER
Sugahara Glass Design
FIRM
Eastern Accent
MANUFACTURER
Sugahara Glass

PRODUCT:
Lotus Wine Glasses
DESIGNER:
Andree Putman
FIRM:
Studio Ecart
MANUFACTURER:
Sasaki Crystal

PRODUCT:
''Classico'' Stemware
DESIGNERS:
Lella and Massimo Vignelli with
David Law
FIRM:
Vignelli Designs
MANUFACTURER:
Sasaki Crystal

PRODUCT:
''Coolers''
DESIGNER:
Brion Sprinsock
FIRM:
Blast
MANUFACTURER:
Blast

PRODUCT:
Drinking Glasses
DESIGNER:
Judy Smilow
FIRM:
Judy Smilow
MANUFACTURER:
Sasaki Crystal

PRODUCT
Cups
DESIGNER
Ikuzi Teraki
FIRM
Romulus Craft
MANUFACTURER
Romulus Craft

PRODUCT:
Geo Glassware
DESIGNER:
Ken Benson
FIRM:
Ahlstrom-Iittala
MANUFACTURER:
Ahlstrom-Iittala

PRODUCT
''Santa Fe'' Martini Set
DESIGNER
Brion Sprinsock
FIRM
Blast
MANUFACTURER
Blast

PRODUCT:
3 Quart Pitcher
DESIGNERS:
Davin Stowell, Annie Breckenfeld,
Brent Markee
FIRM:
Smart Design Inc.

PRODUCT:
''Spinn'' 2
DESIGNER:
Bertil Vallien
FIRM:
Kosta Boda AB, Sweden
MANUFACTURER:
Kosta Boda AB, Sweden
CLIENT:
Kosta Boda AB, Sweden

PRODUCT:
Orion Bowl
DESIGNER:
Llars Hellsten
MANUFACTURER:
AB Orrefors Glasbruk

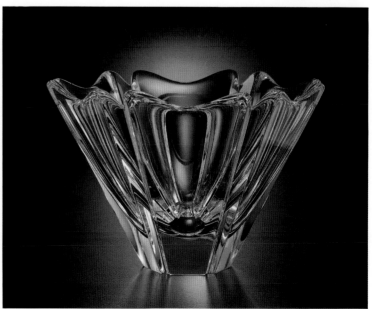

PRODUCT:
''Coco Lezzone'' Dinnerware
DESIGNER:
Paul Steinberg
MANUFACTURER:
Grazia Ceramiche
CLIENT:
Barneys New York

PRODUCT:
''Corinth'' Place Setting
DESIGNER:
Michael Graves
FIRM
Michael Graves, Architect
MANUFACTURER
Swid Powell
CLIENT
Swid Powell

PRODUCT:
Exclusive Tableware For Sointu
DESIGNER:
Ikuzi Teraki
FIRM:
Romulus Craft

PRODUCT:
Three Piece Plate Set Dots and
Dashes
DESIGNER:
Judy Smilow
FIRM:
Judy Smilow
MANUFACTURER:
Judy Smilow

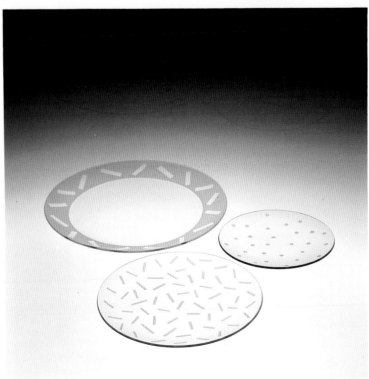

PRODUCT:
Tableware
DESIGNER:
Ann Morhauser
FIRM:
Annie Glass Studio
MANUFACTURER:
Annie Glass Studio

PRODUCT:
Square Platter, Triangle, Dish
DESIGNER:
Robin Drauss
FIRM:
Urbania

PRODUCT:
Plate And Bowl With ''Geta'' Board
DESIGNERS:
Ikuzi Teraki, Jeanne Bisson
FIRM:
Romulus Craft

PRODUCT:
Square Plates With Inner Circle
DESIGNERS:
Ikuzi Teraki, Jeanne Bisson
FIRM:
Romulus Craft

PRODUCT:
"El Jardin" Bowl
DESIGNERS:
Gordon Naylor, Eric Bergman
FIRM:
Neophile
MANUFACTURER:
Neophile

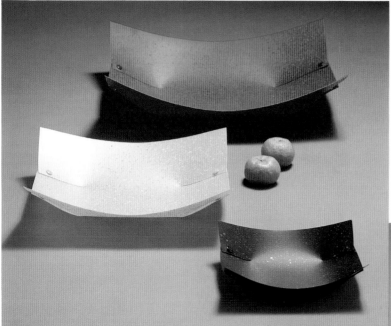

PRODUCT:
Folding Plates and Bowls
DESIGNER:
Tetsuji Kawamura
FIRM:
Gallery 91
MANUFACTURER:
P.P.I.C., Japan
CLIENT:
Gallery 91

PRODUCT:
''Aztec''
DESIGNERS:
Philip Baldwin, Monica Guggisberg
FIRM:
Verrerie De Nonfoux
MANUFACTURER:
Rosenthal AG. Switzerland

PRODUCT
''The Wave''
DESIGNER
Marek Cecula
FIRM
Contemporary Porcelain Gallery
MANUFACTURER
Contemporary Porcelain Gallery

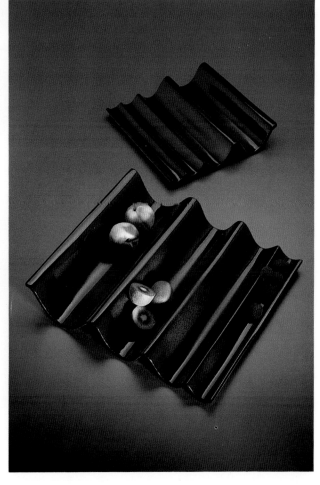

PRODUCT:
Ganymede Bowl
DESIGNER:
David Zelman
FIRM:
Prologue 2000
MANUFACTURER:
Prologue 2000
PHOTO:
Simon Feldman

PRODUCT:
The Chopper and Bowl
DESIGNERS:
Davin Stowell, Annie Breckenfeld
FIRM:
Smart Design, Inc.

PRODUCT:
Dinnerware
DESIGNER:
Daniel Levy
FIRM:
Daniel Levy
MANUFACTURER:
Daniel Levy Ceramics

PRODUCT:
Oval Dish
DESIGNER:
Goran Warff
FIRM:
Kosta Boda, Sweden
MANUFACTURER:
Kosta Boda, Sweden

PRODUCT:
Tabletop Ware
DESIGNER:
Ann Morhauser
FIRM:
Annie Glass Studio
MANUFACTURER:
Annie Glass Studio

PRODUCT:
''Baltic Woods''
DESIGNER:
Ken Benson
FIRM:
Ahlstrom-Iittala, Inc.
MANUFACTURER:
Thaiwood

PRODUCT:
''UFO'' Bowl
DESIGNER:
Gunnel Sahlin
FIRM.
Kosta Boda AB
MANUFACTURER:
Kosta Boda AB, Sweden

PRODUCT
Flower Vase
DESIGNER
Rob Dashorst
FIRM
Daskas
MANUFACTURER
Daskas
CLIENT
Kikkerland Co.

PRODUCT:
''Himalaya''
DESIGNER:
Bertil Vallien
FIRM:
Kosta Boda AB, Sweden
MANUFACTURER:
Kosta Boda AB, Sweden

PRODUCT:
''Sails'' Vase
DESIGNER:
Goran Warff
FIRM:
Kosta Boda AB, Sweden
MANUFACTURER:
Kosta Boda AB, Sweden

PRODUCT:
AG111 Bud Vase/Candlestick
DESIGNER:
Al Glass, Rick Myerchalk
FIRM:
Glass & Glass Inc.
MANUFACTURER:
BDI
CLIENT:
BDI

PRODUCT:
Cultura Metal 4 And 5
DESIGNER:
Ann Wahlstrom
FIRM:
Silver & Stal AB, Sweden
MANUFACTURER:
Silver & Stal AB, Sweden

PRODUCT:
''Gilina'' Flower Pot (Vase)
DESIGNER:
Luciano Devia
FIRM:
Luciano Devia Design Associados,
Brazil
MANUFACTURER:
Alves Pinto Prataria Ltda.

PRODUCT
Corinne Vase
DESIGNER
Clodagh
FIRM
Clodagh, Inc.
MANUFACTURER
Clodagh, Inc.
CLIENT
Prototype

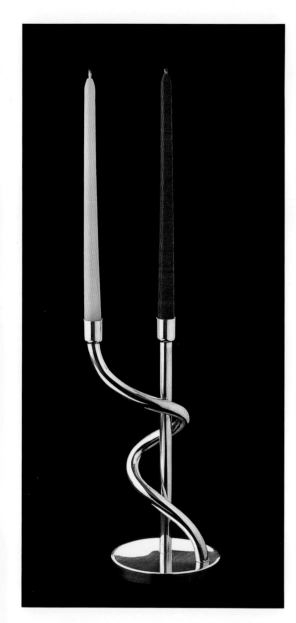

PRODUCT:
''Maga'' Candelabrum
DESIGNER:
Luciano Devia
FIRM:
Luciano Devia Design Associados,
Brazil
MANUFACTURER:
Alves Pinto Prataria Ltda.

PRODUCT
Candle Holder
DESIGNER
David Zelman
FIRM
Prologue 2000
MANUFACTURER
Prologue 2000

PRODUCT:
Candlesticks
DESIGNER:
Jonathan Bonner
CLIENT:
Clodagh, Ross & Williams

PRODUCT
Ghia Candlesticks
DESIGNER
M.A.W. Robinson
FIRM
Detail
MANUFACTURER
Detail Accessories Int'l Inc.

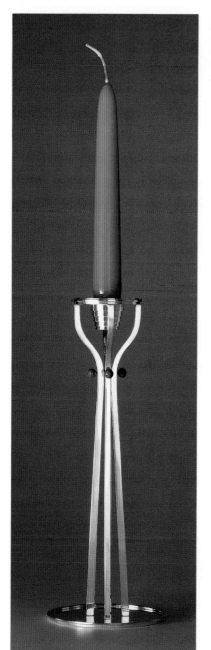

PRODUCT:
Candeliere Tlemcen
DESIGNER:
Paolo Portoghesi
FIRM:
Alessi, Spa

PRODUCT
''Family'' Candlesticks
DESIGNER
Dorothy Hafner
FIRM
Dorothy Hafner

PRODUCT
Candle Holders
DESIGNER
Bravo Basta
FIRM
Eastern Accent
MANUFACTURER
Rhino Stamping
CLIENT
Eastern Accent

PRODUCT
Candlestick, Peppermill, 15''
Serving Tray
DESIGNER
Richard Meier
FIRM
Swid Powell
MANUFACTURER
Swid Powell

PRODUCT:
Macinapepe
DESIGNER:
Michael Graves, Architects
MANUFACTURER:
Alessi

PRODUCT
Soy Sauce Bottle
DESIGNER
Saburo Funakoshi
FIRM
Hoya Corporation
MANUFACTURER
Hoya Musashi Plant

PRODUCT:
Dressing Bottles
DESIGNER:
Saburo Funakoshi
FIRM:
Hoya Corporation
MANUFACTURER:
Hoya Musashi Plant
AWARD:
Long Life Design Prize, Miti, Japan

PRODUCT:
Pepper and Salt
DESIGNER:
Gert-Jan Vogel
FIRM:
Duo Design, The Netherlands
MANUFACTURER:
New Face Design
CLIENT:
Kikkerland Co.

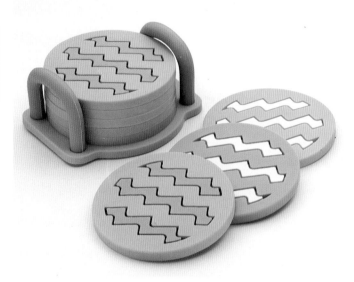

PRODUCT
C312 Coaster Caddy With Six
Coasters
DESIGNER
Paul Rowan
FIRM
Umbra U.S.A. Inc.
MANUFACTURER
Umbra Shades Ltd.

PRODUCT:
Jumbo Jar
DESIGNER:
Annie Breckenfeld
FIRM:
Smart Design, Inc.

PRODUCT
Canisters
DESIGNER
Laura Handler
FIRM
Handler
MANUFACTURER
Hearth And Home Designs By
Creative Ceramics Corp.
CLIENT
McIntyre Associates

PRODUCT
''Gourmet'' Table Service
DESIGNERS
Gemma Bernal, Ramon Isern
FIRM
Bernal/Isern
MANUFACTURER
Innovator S.A.
CLIENT
Innovator S.A.

PRODUCT:
Roller Coasters
DESIGNER:
Lloyd Schwan
FIRM:
Godley & Schwan
MANUFACTURER:
Godley & Schwan

PRODUCT
''Flower Spheres''
DESIGNER
Marek Cecula
FIRM
Contemporary Porcelain Gallery
MANUFACTURER
Contemporary Porcelain Gallery

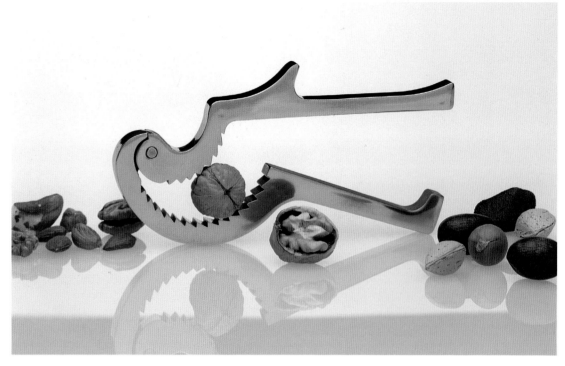

PRODUCT
''Jaws'' Nutcracker
DESIGNER
Marvin Polsfuss
MANUFACTURER
Prodyne

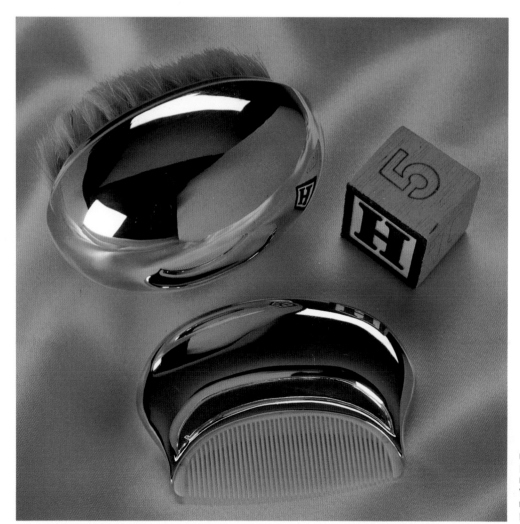

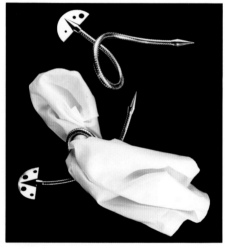

PRODUCT:
''Laocoonte'' Flexible Napkin Holder
DESIGNER:
Titi Cusatelli
MANUFACTURER:
Noto Srl

PRODUCT:
Dressing Table Set
DESIGNER:
Viviana Torun Burlow-Hube
FIRM:
Dansk International Designs Ltd.

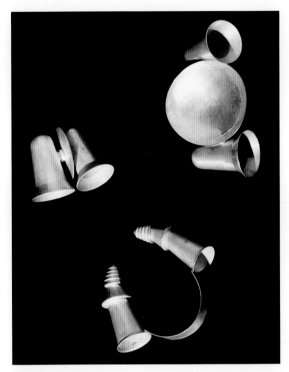

PRODUCT
Chantal SL Fondue Set
DESIGNER
Heida Thurlow
FIRM
Lentrade, Inc.
MANUFACTURER
Lentrade, Inc.

PRODUCT:
''Eatalien'' Sperimental Cutlery To
Be Worn On Fingers
DESIGNER:
Titi Cusatelli
MANUFACTURER:
Noto Srl

PRODUCT:
Culeus Knife
DESIGNERS:
Kazuo Kawasaki
FIRM:
ex-Industrial Design, Inc.
MANUFACTURER:
ex-Industrial Design, Inc., Japan
CLIENT:
Gallery 91
AWARD:
1987 ID Design Review

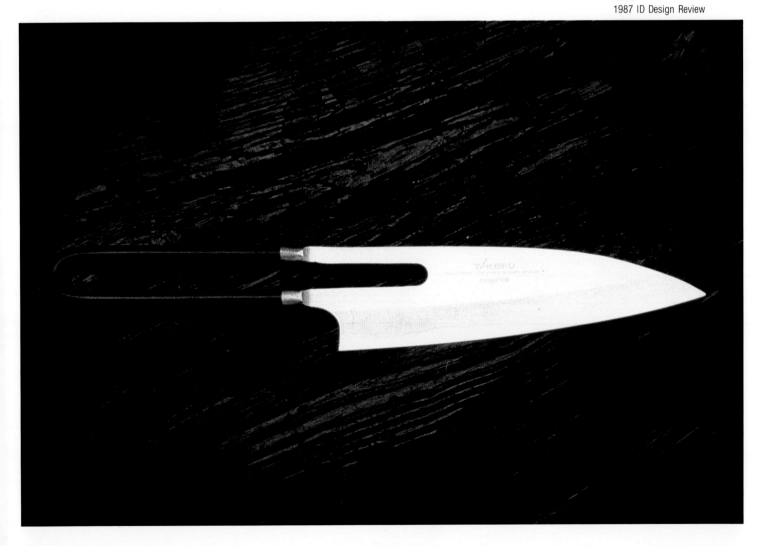

PRODUCT:
Flatware
DESIGNER:
Vivianna Torun Bulow-Hube
FIRM:
Dansk International Designs Ltd.

PRODUCT:
''Next'' Cutlery
DESIGNER:
Bertil Vallein
FIRM:
Boda Nova
MANUFACTURER:
Boda Nova
CLIENT:
Boda Nova

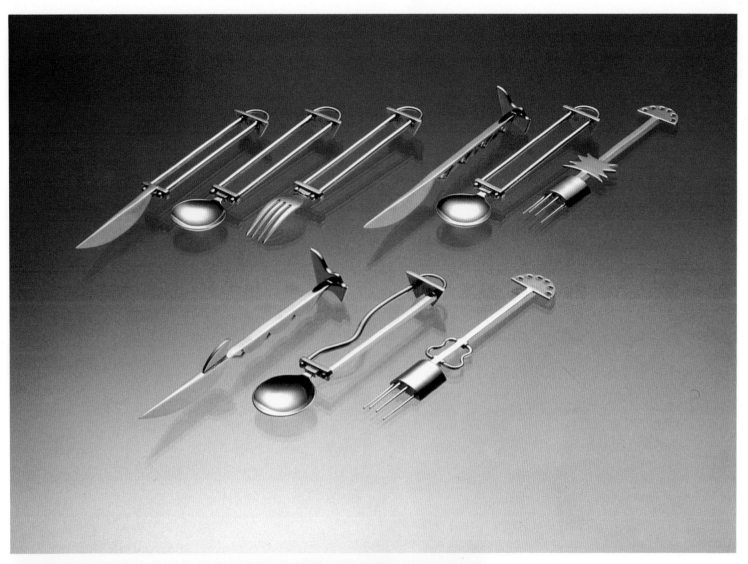

PRODUCT:
''Nobile Produzione'' Flatware
DESIGNER:
Shozo Toyorisa
FIRM:
Eastern Accent
MANUFACTURER:
Koyo Sangyo, Japan
CLIENT:
Eastern Accent

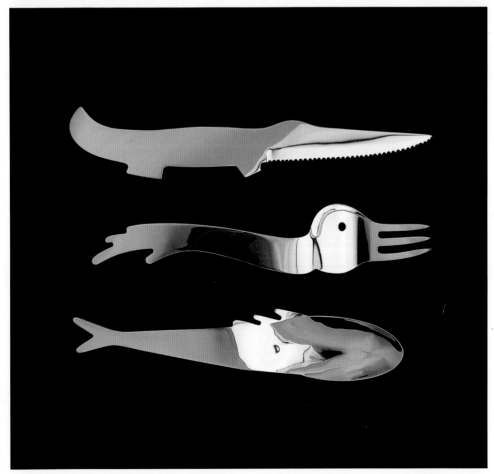

PRODUCT:
''Esotismo'' Flatware
DESIGNER:
Jean-Marie Patois
FIRM:
Creations Jean-Marie Patois, France

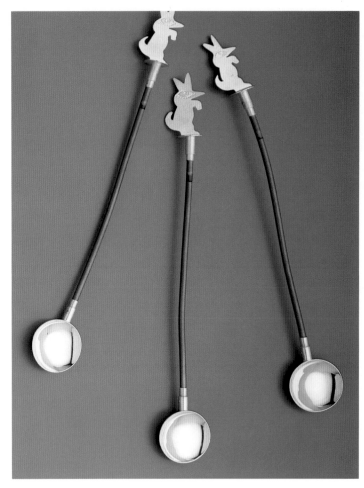

PRODUCT
''Barking Dog Spoons''
DESIGNER
Roy
FIRM
Archetype Gallery
MANUFACTURER
Roy

PRODUCT
Picnic Set
FIRM
Marcovici Design
CLIENT
Museum of Modern Art

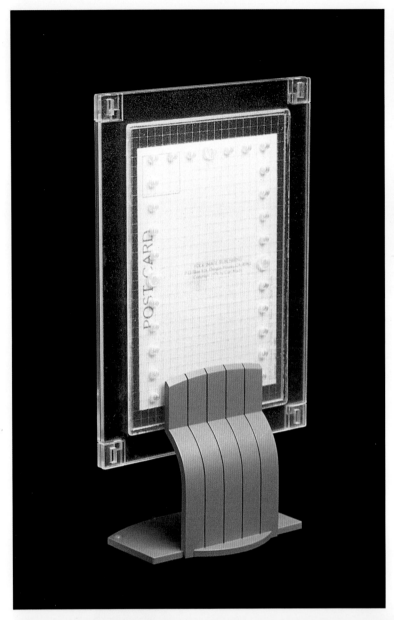

PRODUCT
Snapshot Picture Frames
DESIGNERS
Brian Stewart, Bill Moggridge
FIRM
ID Two

PRODUCT
Geo Frame TM - LC385
DESIGNER
Nicolai Canneti
FIRM
Canneti Inc.
MANUFACTURER
Canneti Inc.
CLIENT
Canneti Inc.
AWARD
1988 ID DESIGN REVIEW

PRODUCT
Picture Frame
DESIGNER
David Tisdale
FIRM
David Tisdale Design Inc.
MANUFACTURER
David Tisdale Design Inc.

PRODUCT
''Flash'' Brunch Service
DESIGNER
Dorothy Hafner
MANUFACTURER
Rosenthal Studio—Linie

PRODUCT
Dressing Table Mirror
DESIGNER
John Chiara
MANUFACTURER
John Chiara

PRODUCT:
Ginger Collection
DESIGNERS:
Davide Marcatali, Paolo Pedrizzetti
FIRM:
Valli Ceramiche, Italy

PRODUCT
"Hollywood White" Crystal
DESIGNER
Monica Backstrom
FIRM
Kosta Boda AB
MANUFACTURER
Kosta Boda AB

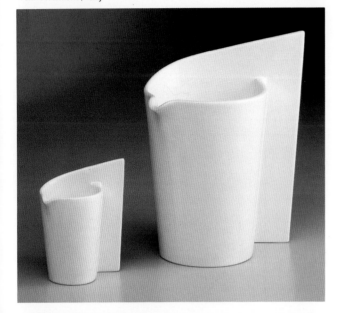

PRODUCT
Teapot and Sugarbowl
DESIGNER
Laura Handler
FIRM
Handler
MANUFACTURER
Pomellato
CLIENT
Pomellato, Inc.
AWARD
Pride of Place Setting, Parsons
School of Design

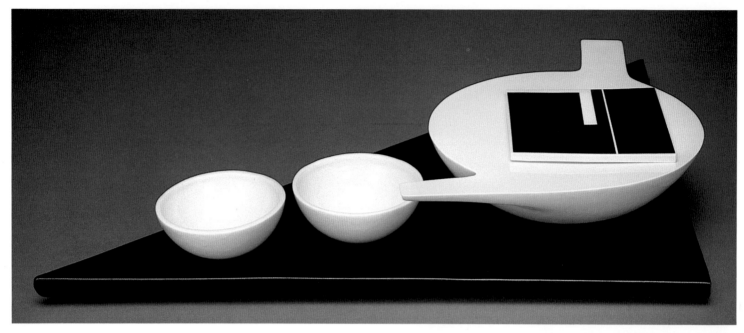

PRODUCT
Ceremonial Set
DESIGNER
Marek Cecula
FIRM
Contemporary Porcelain Gallery
MANUFACTURER
Contemporary Porcelain Studio

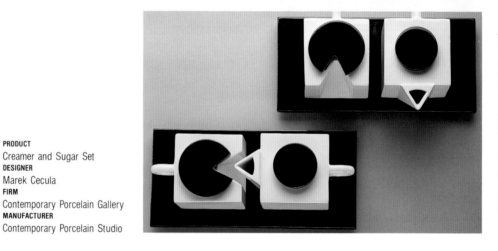

PRODUCT
Creamer and Sugar Set
DESIGNER
Marek Cecula
FIRM
Contemporary Porcelain Gallery
MANUFACTURER
Contemporary Porcelain Studio

PRODUCT
Filter Drip Coffeemaker Service
DESIGNER
Michael Graves
FIRM
Michael Graves, Architect
MANUFACTURER
Swid Powell
CLIENT
Swid Powell

PRODUCT
Tea Service
DESIGNER
Vivianna Torun Bulow-Hube
FIRM
Dansk International Designs Ltd.

PRODUCT
''Cupola White'' Coffee Service
DESIGNER
Mario Bellini
MANUFACTURER
Rosenthal Studio—Linie

PRODUCT
''Cupola White'' Coffee Service
DESIGNER
Mario Bellini
MANUFACTURER
Rosenthal Studio—Linie

CHAPTER 2

William Lansing Plumb
Chairman
Plumb Pearson Inc.

I think my favorite electronic product is Atelier's ADS stereo that Dieter Rams of Braun designed. Part of it is made in the United States, part in Germany and part in Asia. To me, it represents the highest level of design: it's unobtrusive, simple to operate and has very few controls. It's black and very elegant, very understated. All the buttons and dials that are seldom used are hidden under little covers so you don't see them unless you want to operate them. Its modular components all fit together, yet it sits by itself and has its own character. It isn't overwhelmed with a lot of fussy details.

I just bought a Volvo 760 that has the world's most complicated stereo in it. That stereo is an example of terrible design, even though it's very expensive. It has many incomprehensible operations, many controls and buttons that make it very hard just to change the station. It's stupid design. A lot of electronics are, but a lot of them are designed so that when you see them on a shelf, they look important. For example, all these graphic equalizers with a little automated LED or LCD. None of them have much meaning except to exemplify your bad or good taste, and I don't argue taste.

•

There are very few new designs for tape recorders or stereos. George Nelson said years ago that it's part of basic human nature to get bored with things. You want to have something new and fresh and colorful, or if you have too many colorful things, you want something new and fresh in black. That's why Victorian went into Modernism and Modernism evolved to post-Modernism. A lot now also has to do with the media. Most design you read about on the so-called leading edge is. I think, meaningless. Good design is solving a problem. Otherwise it's art. While that's also perfectly legitimate, it's not design. There's nothing wrong with art products. Certainly, no one knows how to draw the lines between craft, design

and art. But design is not for the amusement of the creator. It's for the amusement of the person buying.

For the most part, design is like a hammer and nail, and a hammer and nail don't change very much. No industrial designer I know has ever designed a nail. On a hammer, you can only redesign the handle a bit, probably manipulate it from the head. If I want to drive a nail, I want a serious hammer. I want an extension of my mind that is going to help me do something or communicate. I'm not interested in fashion. Take for example, hearing aids. How many people wear decorative hearing aids? I've never seen one.

•

Design for the handicapped is really important because it allows disabled people to physically do things they wouldn't be able to do otherwise. A lot of design in computers and telecommunications is also functional because it's extending your brain and allowing you to use things instead of just to decorate your house. So now design is becoming a process through which your mind can find new meaning, new extensions, new possibilities. That's where the most important work is being done.

In the future, I see electronics merging with computer technology and the result will affect the way people live. The electronic home is coming. The Japanese are soon going to have television sets with minicomputers in them. You'll see the merging of computers and television in the Read Only Memory-CD. This will be a database source in which one CD-ROM—which is the same size as a regular CD—will hold some 200,000 pages of text or the equivalent of the *Encyclopaedia Brittanica*. You'll be able to put that into your disc player and hook up the computer and have information you can interact with via the TV. This will blur the line between computers. entertainment. and education.

•

Not too long ago, I had a discussion with an old associate of mine. He said that "design occurs only after you sit down at the drawing board and begin to put the pencil to the paper. The rest of it is meaningless." And I didn't agree because, frankly, there are lots of talented young people who can render or manipulate a computer to create a zippy-looking product. That's the easy part. The real questions are, what are the choices you make before you sit down? What do you want to say or do? Do you even have an idea?

•

Thanks to the micro-chip, you can now design a product into any form you want. You can make a computer that looks like a banana. You can do this because the computer's form is unrelated to its electro-mechanical side. In the old days, Italian design was based on the idea of making electro-mechanics express function. But now that there is nothing but a chip and a few wires, how do you express that? You can't. So you have to express something else, and designers are having a hard time figuring that out. It's harder and more elusive and in many respects there are fewer opportunities to express an egocentric point of view. In a way, the chip has made design less exclusive and more democratic.

Consequently, you see limited production companies like Swid-Powell turning to architects, like Michael Graves and Robert Venturi, who design dinnerwear using stock patterns with different graphic decorations. And it's all hype. For Christmas, I bought a Richard Meier key chain for my wife, and very soon after. this badly-made silver ring broke and had to be replaced with a 25-cent ring from the hardware store. You realize that this is not design. This is...well...I have an expression which some people don't like...it's stupid design and it gives the field a bad name. Often what they do is fashion. It's society. It's *Town and Country*.

PRODUCT
Watches
DESIGNER
Systema Corp.
FIRM
Eastern Accent
MANUFACTURER
Systema Corp.

PRODUCT
Digital Tape Player
DESIGNERS
Thomas Bley, Jorg Ratzlaff
FIRM
Zebra Design
MANUFACTURER
Zebra Design

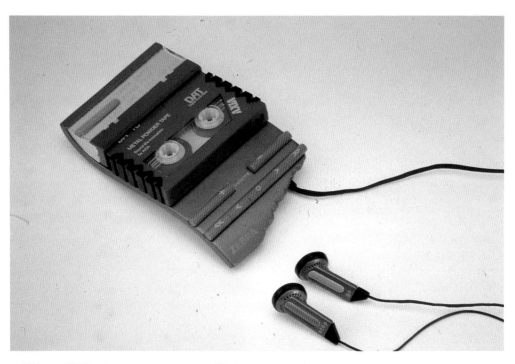

PRODUCT
''My First Sony'' Products
DESIGNER
Sony Design Center
FIRM
Sony Corporation
MANUFACTURER
Sony Japan .

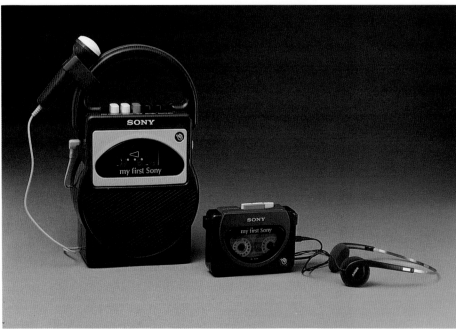

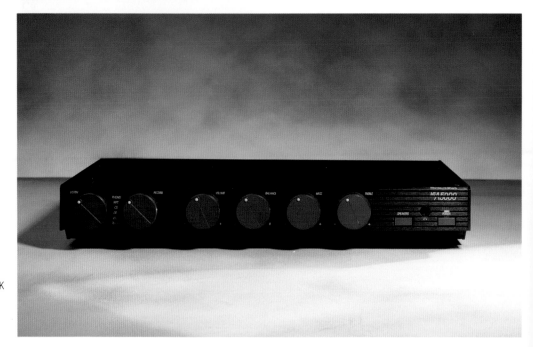

PRODUCT
Mordaunt-Short A5000 Amplifier
DESIGNER
Stephen Williams
FIRM
Roberts Weaver Design Limited, UK
MANUFACTURER
TGI Group Ltd.
CLIENT
TGI Group Ltd.

PRODUCT
Stereo—Concept
DESIGNER
Chris Barlow

PRODUCT
WM-109 Personal Stereo Cassette
Player
DESIGNER
Sony Design Center
FIRM
Sony Corporation
MANUFACTURER
Sony Japan

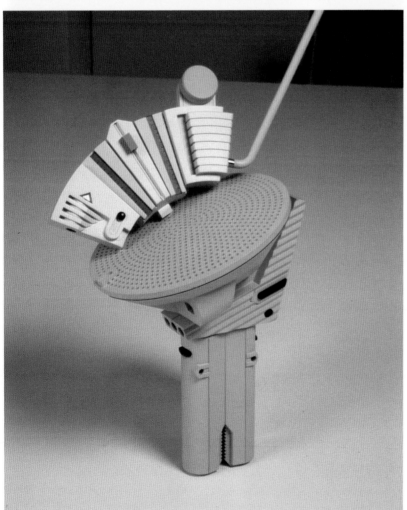

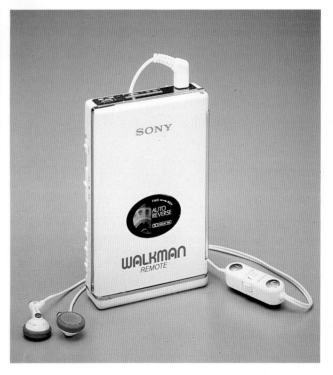

PRODUCT
FM/AM Radio – Concept
DESIGNER
Richard Appleby
FIRM
Atlantic Design
DESCRIPTION
Parts can be disassembled and
reconfigured.

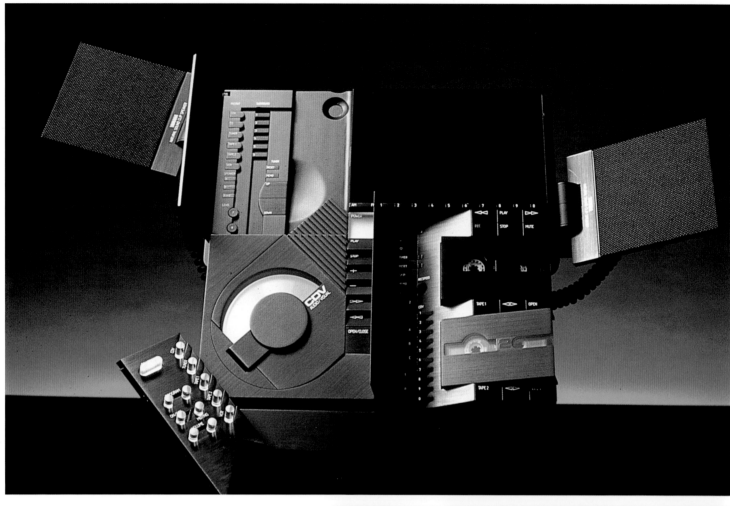

PRODUCT
AVOT Audio & Visual Equipment
Concept
DESIGNER
Product Design Department
FIRM
GK Inc.
MANUFACTURER
Yamaha Corp.
CLIENT
Yamaha Corp.

PRODUCT
Boston Acoustics Designer Series
Model 360 Loudspeaker
DESIGNER
Charles Rozier
FIRM
Charles Rozier Design
MANUFACTURER
Boston Acoustics, Inc.
CLIENT
Boston Acoustics, Inc.
AWARD
1987 Summer Consumer Electronics
Show, Chicago

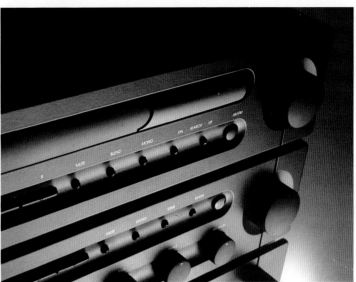

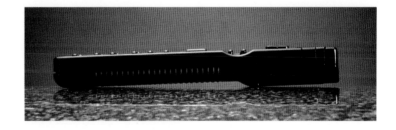

PRODUCT
Soundstream System 1
DESIGNERS
Doug Patton, Matthew Duncan,
Richard Jung, Joan Ciranny
FIRM
Patton Design Enterprises
MANUFACTURER
Soundstream
CLIENT:
Soundstream

PRODUCT
RL 60.2 Loud Speaker
DESIGNER
David Lewis
FIRM
David Lewis Designs
MANUFACTURER
Bang & Olufsen A/S
CLIENT
Bang & Olufsen A/S
AWARD:
1986 ID Design Review

PRODUCT
VCR 2
DESIGNER
Fischerdesignteam
FIRM
Fischerdesignteam
MANUFACTURER
Go Video Inc.
CLIENT
Go Video Inc.

PRODUCT
Citation 23 Active Tracking Tuner
Citation 21 Control Preamplifier
DESIGNERS
Daniel Ashcraft, Dan Wickemeyer
FIRM
Ashcraft Design
MANUFACTURER
Harman/Kardon
CLIENT
Harman America

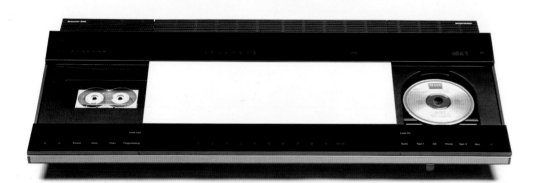

PRODUCT
Beosystem 9000
DESIGNER
Jakob Jensen
FIRM
Jakob Jensen
MANUFACTURER
Bang & Olufsen A/S
CLIENT
Bang & Olufsen A/S
AWARD
1988 ID Design Review

PRODUCT
Powered Partners Speaker System
DESIGNERS
Richard Elliot Randell, Carol Rhodes
Catalano, Domenic Giuntoli
FIRM
Gregory Fossela Design, Inc.
AWARD
1987 ID Design Review, 1987 IDEA
Award

PRODUCT:
Emu Systems Emulator III
DESIGNER:
Robert Brunner
FIRM:
Lunar Design Incorporated
MANUFACTURER:
Emu Systems
CLIENT:
Emu Systems

PRODUCT
Electric Guitar
DESIGNER
Seymour:Powell
FIRM
Seymour:Powell
CLIENT
Seymour:Powell
AWARD
1988 ID Design Review

PRODUCT
Control 3 Pro – Personal Sized
Monitor Loudspeaker
DESIGNERS
Daniel Ashcraft, Dan Wickemeyer
FIRM
Ashcraft Design
MANUFACTURER
JBL Incorporated
CLIENT
JBL International

PRODUCT
Speakers
DESIGNER
Jakob Jensen
FIRM
Jakob Jensen
MANUFACTURER
Bang & Olufsen A/S
CLIENT
Bang & Olufsen A/S

PRODUCT
Zanuso Telephone
DESIGNER
Marco Zanusco
FIRM
Zanuso Design
CLIENT
Becker, Inc.

PRODUCT
Digital Answering Machine
Concepts
DESIGNERS
D.M. Gresham, Martin Thaler,
James Ludwig
FIRM
Design Logic
CLIENT
Dictaphone, Inc.

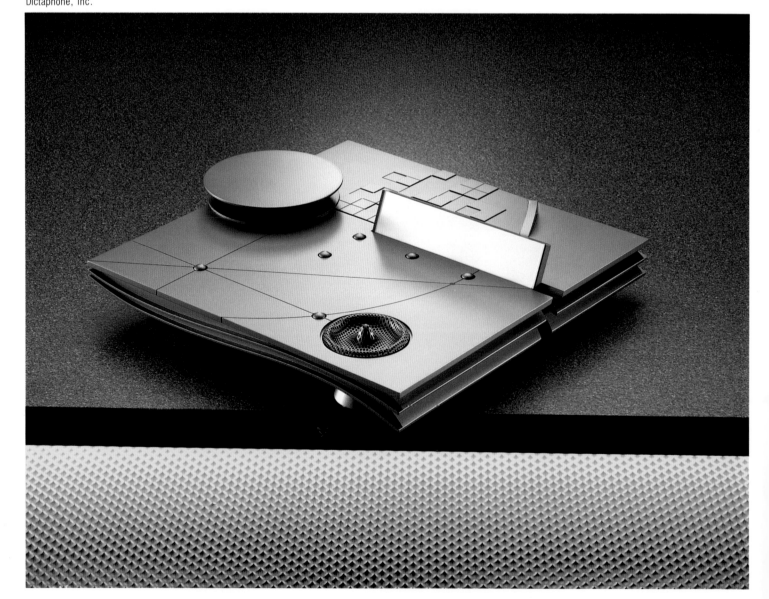

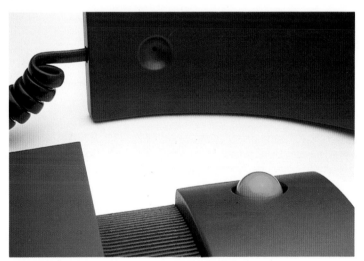

PRODUCT
''Phonebook'' Telephone Answering
Machine Concept
DESIGNER
Lisa Krohn
FIRM
Smart Design
AWARDS
1987 Forma Finlandia, 1987 ID
Design Review, Frog Junior 1987

PRODUCT
Voice Dialer
DESIGNERS
Nelson Au, Michel Nuttall
FIRM
Matrix Product Design Inc.
CLIENT
Innovative Devices
PHOTOGRAPHER
Rick English

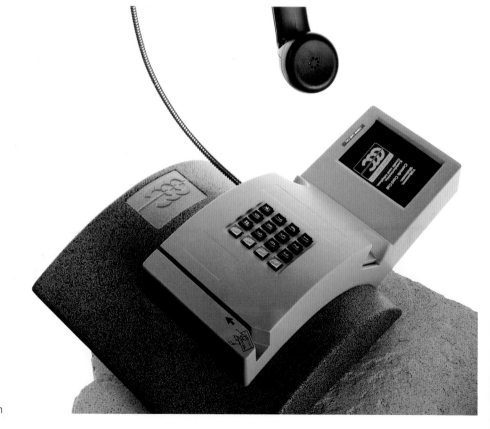

PRODUCT
Credit Card Telephone
DESIGNER
Hartmut Esslinger
FIRM
frogdesign
MANUFACTURER
Comvik Card Call AB, Sweden

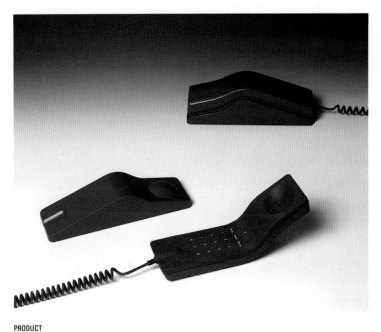

PRODUCT
Becker EC Phone
DESIGNER
Eric P. Chan
FIRM
Chan + Dolan Industrial Design Inc.
MANUFACTURER
Becker Inc.
CLIENT
Becker Inc.

PRODUCT
System Phone
DESIGNER
Paul Bradley
FIRM
Matrix Product Design Inc.
CLIENT
Tsunami

PRODUCT
Attendant Console
DESIGNER
Martin Darbyshire
FIRM
ID TWO
CLIENT
Telenova Inc.
DESCRIPTION
The LCD display can be adjusted by
tilting housing to suit operator.

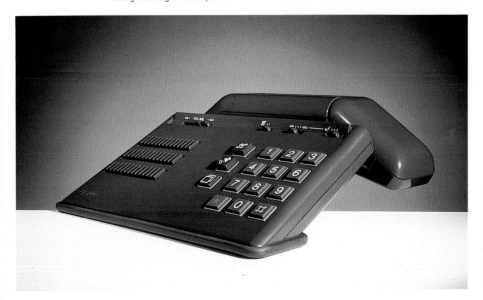

PRODUCT
Grazia Telephone
DESIGNER
Mario Bellini
FIRM
NNT, Japan
AWARD
Good Design Awards for Minestry &
Commerce

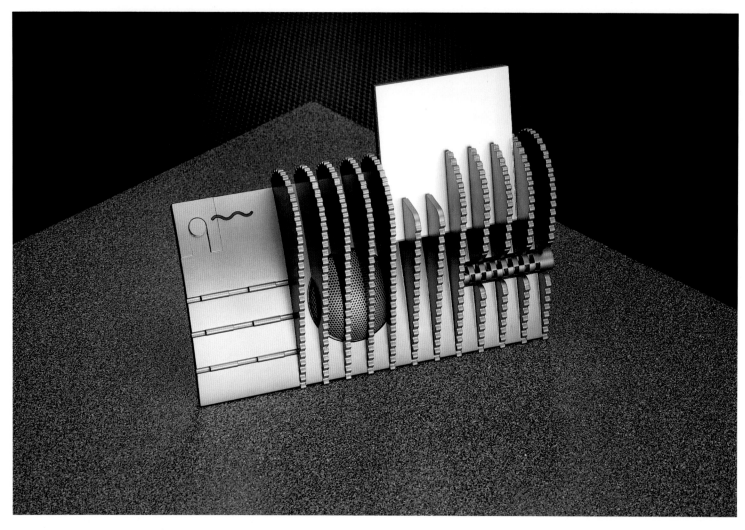

PRODUCT:
Digital Phone Answering Machine –
Concept
DESIGNERS:
D.M. Gresham, Martin Thaler,
James Ludwig
FIRM:
Design Logic
CLIENT:
Dictaphone, Inc.

PRODUCT
RD9XL – Radar Detector
DESIGNER
James K. Langford
FIRM:
Uniden Corporation of America
MANUFACTURER:
Uniden Corporation of America
CLIENT:
Uniden Corporation of America
DESCRIPTION:
The world's smallest radar detector.
Dimensions: 2 5/32'' x 1/2'' x
11/16''

PRODUCT
Field Telephone
DESIGNER
Seymour:Powell
FIRM
Seymour:Powell
MANUFACTURER
Racal
CLIENT
Racal

PRODUCT:
Dancall 5000
DESIGNERS:
John Stoddard, Nick Dormon,
Charles Ash
FIRM:
Moggridge Associates
CLIENT:
Dancall Radio A/S
AWARD:
Design Innovation '88, Haus
Industrieform Essen

PRODUCT
AP 4115/4112 NMT Mobile
Telephone
DESIGNERS
Jan Tragardh, Niels Christiansen
FIRM
Philips Industri

PRODUCT
Radar Detector
DESIGNER
Jeffrey Heuel
FIRM
Contours Consulting Design Group
Inc.
MANUFACTURER
Cobra/Div. of Dynascan Corporation
CLIENT
Cobra/Dynascan

PRODUCT
Radar Detector
DESIGNERS
John Hui, Hari Matsuda
FIRM
Hari and Associates
MANUFACTURER:
Whistler Corporation
CLIENT
Whistler Corporation
AWARD
Consumer Electronics Show –
Design & Engineering Excellence
Award

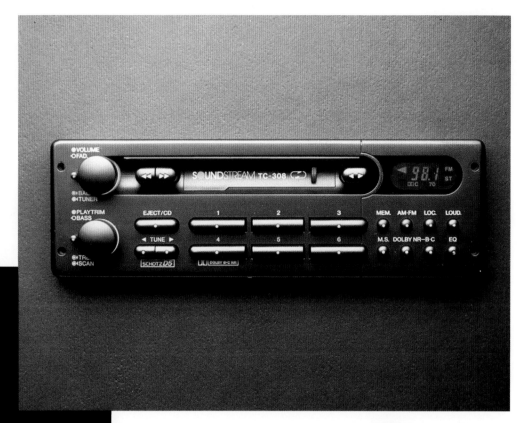

PRODUCT
TC-308 Radio/Tape Deck
DESIGNERS
Doug Patton, Matthew Duncan,
Richard Jung, Joan Ciranny
FIRM
Patton Design Enterprises
MANUFACTURER
Soundstream
CLIENT
Soundstream
AWARDS
1987 ID Design Review Selection,
1988 Grand Prix Autosound Design
Excellence, 1988 American
Corporate Identity Selection
DESCRIPTION
A radio/tape deck designed to be
easily removed and re-attached.

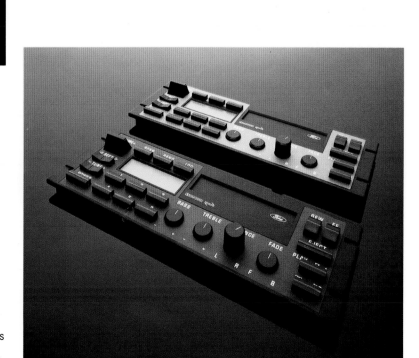

PRODUCT
Premium Radio
DESIGNER
John Stoddard
FIRM
Moggridge Associates
CLIENT
Ford Motor Company

PRODUCT
Pie Watch
DESIGNER
Alexander Brebner
FIRM
M&Co.
MANUFACTURER
M&Co. Labs.
CLIENT
M&Co.

PRODUCT
Time Gauge Watch
DESIGNER
Frank Nichols
FIRM
Design Frame

PRODUCT
Harman/Kardon High Fidelity
Receiver/Deck CR151
DESIGNERS
Daniel Ashcraft, Dan Wickemeyer
FIRM
Ashcraft Design
MANUFACTURER:
Harman/Kardon
CLIENT
Harman America

PRODUCT
Askew Watch
DESIGNERS
Tibor Kalman, Alexander Isley
FIRM
M&Co.
MANUFACTURER
M&Co. Labs
CLIENT
M&Co.
AWARD
1986 International Design Yearbook

PRODUCT
Watch
DESIGNERS
Tibor Kalman, Maria Kalman,
Alexander Isley
FIRM
M&Co.
MANUFACTURER
M&Co. Labs
CLIENT:
M&Co.
AWARD
MOMA Permanent Design Collection,
STA 100, ADLA

PRODUCT
KX-27HV1 25'' Monitor Television
DESIGNER
Sony Design Center
FIRM
Sony Corporation
MANUFACTURER
Sony Japan

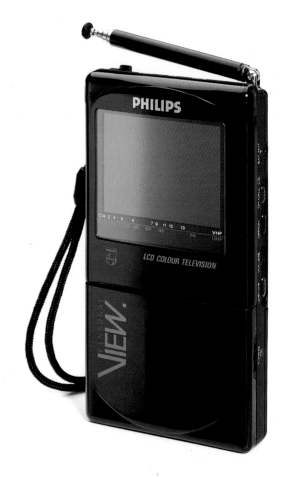

PRODUCT
Philips LCD Color Television
DESIGNER
Philips Corporate Industrial Design
FIRM
Philips Corporation, The Netherlands

PRODUCT
Compact Television Set TH-8U1
DESIGNER
Kyushu Matsushita Electric
Industrial Co., Ltd. Industrial Design
Department
FIRM
Matsushita Electric Industrial Co.,
Ltd.

PRODUCT
Scientific Calculator
DESIGNER
Khodi Feiz
FIRM
Texas Instruments Design Center

PRODUCT
Sekonic Digital Exposure Meter
L-328
DESIGNER
Michiro Kuriyama
FIRM
KAK Design Inc.
MANUFACTURER
Sekonic Co., Ltd.
CLIENT
Sekonic Co., Ltd.

PRODUCT
Olympus Infinity Superzoom 300
DESIGNER
Olympus Corporation
FIRM
Olympus Corporation

PRODUCT
Spectra System Instant Camera
DESIGNERS
James M. Conner, James M. Ryan,
Enrique Alie
FIRM
Henry Dreyfuss Associates
MANUFACTURER
Polaroid Corporation
CLIENT
Polaroid Corporation
AWARD
IDEA Design Achievement Certificate

PRODUCT
BVW-505 Betacam VTR in Camera
Combo
DESIGNER
Sony Design Center
FIRM
Sony Corporation
MANUFACTURER
Sony Japan

PRODUCT
VHS-C Camera Recorder
NV-MC10
DESIGNER
Matsushita Electric Industrial Co.,
Ltd.
Video Recorder Division
FIRM
Matsushita Electric Industrial Co.,
Ltd.

PRODUCT
Canon E-70
DESIGNER
Canon Inc.
FIRM
Canon Inc.

PRODUCT
VX-S405 Camcorder
FIRM
Olympus Corporation

CHAPTER 3

FURNITURE

Ettore Sottsass
Founder
Sottsass Associati

Design is so prevalent today because we lead a life of total communication, and design is one way of communicating. That's why fashion also has such immense importance—because everybody needs to design himself and communicate an idea of himself to others. And the possibility of creating an environment through objects is an idea that in ancient times, only kings could entertain. Now, almost everybody can do it because there has been a certain democratization through design.

I consider good design anything that transmits an idea with an historical and anthropological balance. It is something that fits the context of the future—not the present—a future built on the necessities that people hope to have. Of course, we are always looking back to the past for old metaphors to create new ones.

•

I think that functionalism has lost the meaning that the Bauhaus had originally given it. And Memphis, which allows the surface to send more sensorial information and then tries to separate the object from its schematic idea of functionalism, in a way is an ironic approach to this notion of philosophical pureness. I mean, a table may need four legs to function, but there is no one who can tell me that the four legs have to be the same.

Of course, function is important, but it's not the final word because you can never precisely define the function of an object. Sometimes the object is so simple the function is built into it. I mean a table has to have a certain height and width. So does a chair.

Functionalism is never a cure and it doesn't simply mean ergonomics. Its definition has to be enlarged because objects are functional to life; they are not functional to functions. People respond to things in terms of their own cultural values—physically, financially and psychologically. To a blind man, for example, a pair of glasses has no function. And whenever I

go to these big modern luxury hotels, I never know how or where to sit, and the colors and decorations make me uncomfortable. So in the end, everything there is non-functional for me because my life doesn't need this kind of imagery, adventure, or theater.

•

I don't have one design of my own that I like more than others because I have never looked to build a monument. I feel that all the designs I have done throughout my life are just notes about what one could do without seeking a final definition. Every object is part of the next, like the bricks of a house, if there will ever be a house. They are brief moments of a long journey.

I take inspiration from every event that isn't bound up with institutional culture. For instance, through literature and history, we know a lot about Greek culture, and you can't separate its architecture from the notions you have about Greek social structure. On the other hand, we know very little about the Sumarians, so what I see of that culture is fresh and detached from preconceived ideas. It's inspirational because the images are very pure. It's like going to bed with someone for one night —there is no past and no future. It's just there for one moment, and it is not yet systematized.

•

I suppose that some might say that my work has a playful, childlike quality to it. The child is supposed to be more free psychologically and creatively than an adult. A child's imagination needs very little stimulation because it isn't conditioned by Institutional structures. He or she can see a piece of paper and imagine it to be an airplane, and at times, this state can be recommunicated. I don't think it's a mistake if you tell people to go back to a smile, to go back to something they enjoy that isn't too complicated.

I was very criticized for example, for my use of color. It's risky to try to recover childhood because the whole system is

built on very strict laws about behavior. It's the same with a system of color—objects *should* be black or grey. It's a risk to break away from this system.

•

There are many things I like about being a designer. It's what I have always wanted to do. It's a profession that involves groups of people, and it's not as solitary as painting or poetry. And you deal very much with social problems. A real designer always has technology and production in mind and that's how he differs from an artist. Anytime I design, I consider three things: can it stand up, can it be produced, and will it stay together. So it's a very sophisticated profession, if you want it to be.

I'm not an inventor because I'm more interested in the method of doing things than the final result. And I'm not solving problems because no one solves problems —instead, I am discussing them.

•

What's more interesting, me or my work? I don't think you can necessarily divide the two. You work because you are yourself and you are yourself because you work—I am myself when I design and I don't call it working. When I cannot do something, I feel desperate, like I am losing contact with life. My anxiety about always having to design something is still very strong.

•

What do you think is the signature design for the '80s?
You shouldn't ask me.
Why not?
Because it's Memphis.

PRODUCT
Folding Filly Chair
DESIGNER
Canetti Group
FIRM
Canetti Inc.
MANUFACTURER
Teknoplast
CLIENT
Canetti Inc.

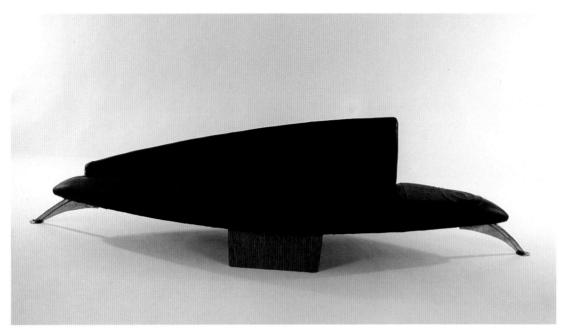

PRODUCT
''Slice'' Sofa
DESIGNER
Alex Locadia
FIRM
Art et Industrie
MANUFACTURER
Art et Industrie/Alex Locadia

PRODUCT
''Juan'' Chaise Lounge
DESIGNERS
Marco Zanini, Aldo Cibic, Ettore
Sottsass
MANUFACTURER
Memphis
CLIENT
Memphis

PRODUCT
''Flying Carpet'' Chair
DESIGNER
Aimon Desanta
FIRM
Casaform
MANUFACTURER
Rosenthal Einrichtung

PRODUCT
Luck
DESIGNER
Toshiyuki Kita
FIRM
Atelier International, Ltd.
MANUFACTURER
Atelier International, Ltd.

PRODUCT
''Vanity Fair''
FIRM
Archivo Frau
Poltrona Frau, S.P.A.

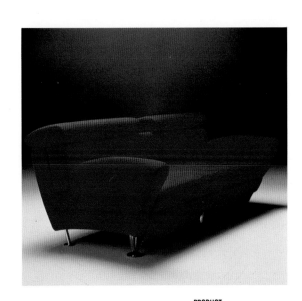

PRODUCT
Balzo 5 Sofa
DESIGNER
Massimo Josa-Ghini
FIRM
Palazetti Inc.
MANUFACTURER
Palazetti Inc.

PRODUCT
Chair
DESIGNER
Fred Baier
FIRM
Fred Baier & Tim Wells

PRODUCT
"Casablanca" Armchair and Sofa
DESIGNER
Jaime Tresserra Clapes
FIRM
J. Tresserra Design
MANUFACTURER
J. Tresserra Design
CLIENT
J. Tresserra Design

PRODUCT
"Futura 3" Chaise Lounge
DESIGNER
Massimo Josa-Ghini
FIRM
Palazzetti Inc.
MANUFACTURER
Palazzetti Inc.

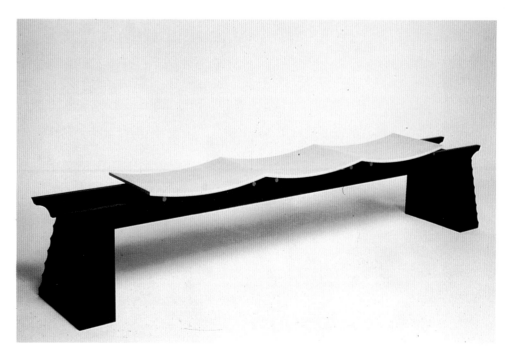

PRODUCT
Bench 93
DESIGNER
Gail Fredell Smith
FIRM
Snyderman Gallery
MANUFACTURER
Snyderman Gallery

PRODUCT
''Prince De Fribourg Et Theyer''
Armchair and Sofa
DESIGNER
Philippe Starck
FIRM
Aleph

PRODUCT
''Agevole'' Armchairs and Sofas
DESIGNER
Ugo La Pietra
FIRM
Gruppo Industriale Busnelli, S.P.A.
MANUFACTURER
Gruppo Industriale Busnelli, S.P.A.

PRODUCT
Bugatti Club Chair
DESIGNER
Franny Romero
FIRM
De Sede of Switzerland
CLIENT
De Sede of Switzerland and Stendig
International
AWARD
1987 ID Design Review Selection

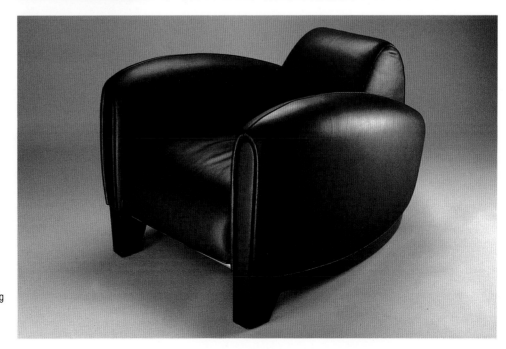

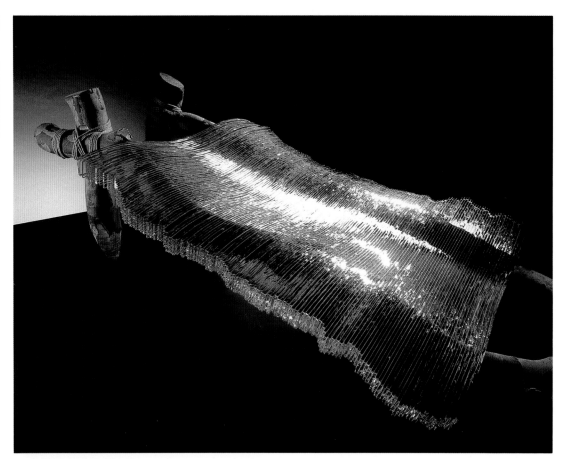

PRODUCT
Angaraib Rope Bed
DESIGNER
Danny Lane
FIRM
Glassworks
PHOTOGRAPHER
Peter Wood

PRODUCT
Pool Chair With Wave Seat
DESIGNERS
Steven Holt, Tucker Viemeister, Lisa Krohn
FIRM
Smart Design
PHOTOGRAPHER
Paul Sciacca
AWARD
1987 ID Design Review

PRODUCT
High Chair
DESIGNER
Rene Van der Vooren
FIRM
Studio Grys
MANUFACTURER
New Face Design
CLIENT
Kikkerland Co.
PHOTO
Bill Orcutt

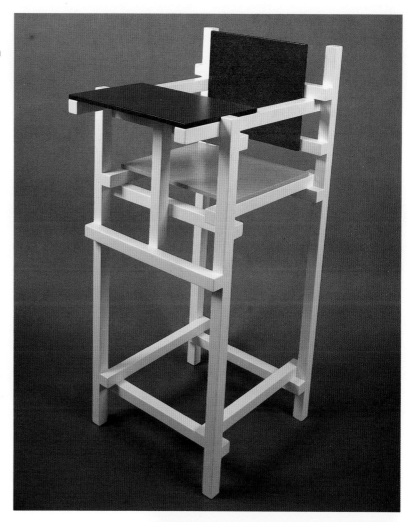

PRODUCT
Ischia Chair
DESIGNERS
Loyd Moore, Dave Gilpin
FIRM
Technology Design

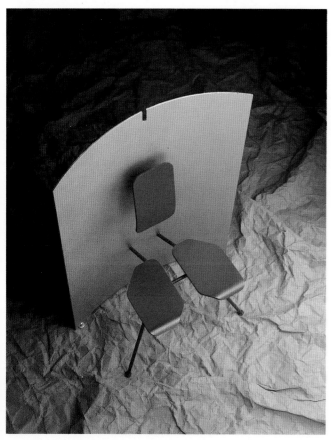

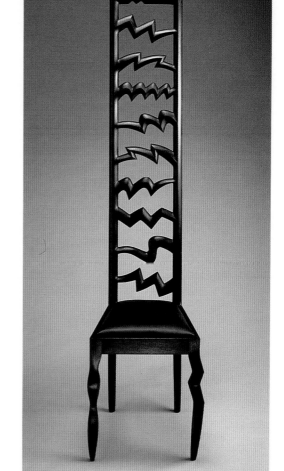

PRODUCT
Ladderback Chair
DESIGNER
Peter Pierobon
FIRM
Snyderman Gallery
MANUFACTURER
Snyderman Gallery
CLIENT
Cinetrix, Canada
PHOTO
Tom Brummett

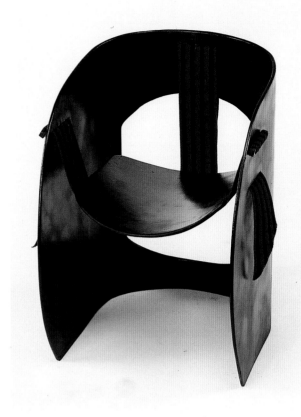

PRODUCT
Stacking ''Womb'' Chair
DESIGNER
Daniel T. Ebihara
FIRM
Gallery 91

PRODUCT
''Off The Wall''
DESIGNER
Kiyoshi Kanai
FIRM
Kiyoshi Kanai Studio
MANUFACTURER
Kiyoshi Kanai Studio

PRODUCT
Anebo Tak Chair
DESIGNER
Borek Sipek
MANUFACTURER
Driade, Italy

PRODUCT
Chair
DESIGNER
Philippe Starck
MANUFACTURER
Driade

PRODUCT
Moform Chair
DESIGNER
Hannu Kahonen
FIRM
Creadesign KY
MANUFACTURER
Moform OY

PRODUCT
Spring Rocker
DESIGNER
Ron Arad
CLIENT
See, Ltd.

PRODUCT
Easy Chair
DESIGNER
Shigeru Uchida
FIRM
Studio 80, Japan
MANUFACTURER
BUILD Co., Ltd.
PHOTO
T. Nacasa & Partners
AWARD
1987 ID Design Review

PRODUCT
BEATO Armchair and Divan
DESIGNERS
Perry King, Santiago Mirando
FIRM
King-Miranda Associati
MANUFACTURER
Disform, Spain
CLIENT
Disform

PRODUCT
''Tokyo'' Chair
DESIGNERS
Roberto Marcatti, Alfonso Crotti
FIRM
Lavori In Corso
MANUFACTURER
Lavori In Corso, Italy

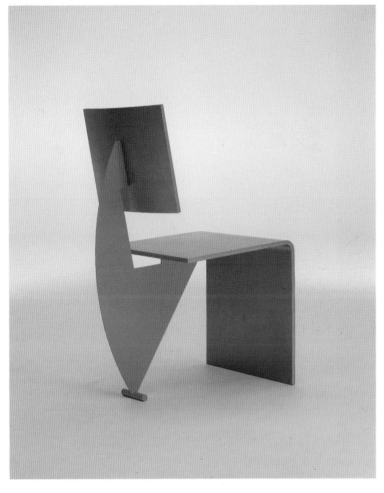

PRODUCT
Chair #2
DESIGNER
Shigeru Uchida
FIRM
Studio 80
CLIENT
Gallery 91
PHOTO
T. Nacasa & Partners

PRODUCT
"Imperial" Rollerchair
DESIGNER
Christoph Boeninger, IDSA, VDID
MANUFACTURER
InterProfil, Contract Division, W.
Germany
AWARD
1987 Interior Design Magazine
Design Selection

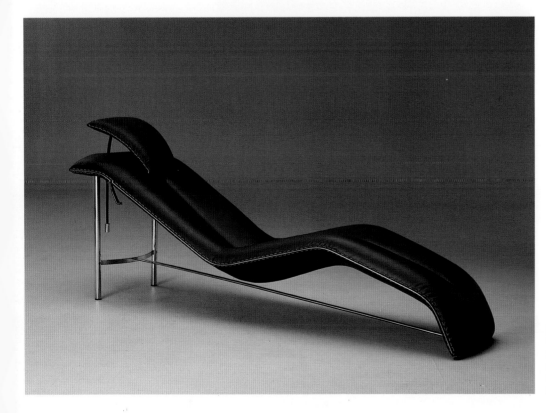

PRODUCT
MILOS Relax Couch
DESIGNER
C. dell'Orso
MANUFACTURER
Strassle Sohne AG, Switzerland

PRODUCT
L.A. Folding Chair
DESIGNER
Christoph Boeninger, IDSA, VDID
MANUFACTURER
mobilia collection, W. Germany
AWARDS
1987 Casa and Interni Magazines
Design Selection

PRODUCT
Academy Chair
DESIGNER
Tom Deacon
FIRM
Area Design, Inc., Toronto
Whomever

PRODUCT
''Montana'' Chairs
DESIGNER
Paul Ludick
MANUFACTURER
Furniture of the 20th Century

PRODUCT
Tarzan Stackable Chair
DESIGNERS
Davide Mercatali, Paolo Pedrizzetti
FIRM
Davide Mercatali, Milan
MANUFACTURER
NOTO, Milan

PRODUCT
''Giocasta'' Armchair
DESIGNER
Roberto Marcatti
FIRM
Lavori In Corso
MANUFACTURER
Lavori In Corso

PRODUCT
''Gazelle'' Chair
DESIGNER
Jonathan Crinion
FIRM
AREA Design Inc.
CLIENT
AREA, Toronto
AWARD
1988 ID Design Review Selection

PRODUCT
3 Stools
DESIGNER
Leslie A. Gubitos
FIRM
Swanke Hayden Connell Architects
MANUFACTURER
Leslie A. Gubitos
AWARD
1988 ID Design Review Selection

PRODUCT
''Frenesi'' Stool
FIRM
Transatlantic, Barcelona
MANUFACTURER
Akaba, S.A.
AWARD
1986 Silver Delta DIA/FAD

PRODUCT
''Mooncycles'' Stools/Pedestals
DESIGNER
Terence Main
FIRM
Art et Industrie
MANUFACTURER
Art et Industrie/Terence Main

PRODUCT
Rubber Stacking Chair
DESIGNER
Brian Kane
FIRM
Metropolitan Furniture Corporation
MANUFACTURER
Metropolitan Furniture Corporation
AWARDS
1987 IBD Honorable Mention, 1987
Resource Council Commendation,
1988 ID Design Review Award

PRODUCT
Sensor
DESIGNER
Wolfgang Muller-Deisig
FIRM
Design Studio Muller-Deisig/
Steelcase Inc.
MANUFACTURER
Steelcase Inc.
AWARD
IBD – Silver

PRODUCT
Cota Serie Office Chairs
DESIGNER
Quod
FIRM
Quod, Disseny i Marketing, S.A.
MANUFACTURER
Galo/Ben
CLIENT
Galo/Ben

PRODUCT
Writing Desk #2
DESIGNER
Jordi Vilanova
FIRM
Jordi Vilanova, S.A.
MANUFACTURER
Jordi Vilanova, S.A., Spain

PRODUCT
Step 1
DESIGNER
Toshyuki Kita
MANUFACTURER
airon, Italy

PRODUCT
Vuelta Reception Table
DESIGNERS
Perry King, Santiago Miranda
FIRM
King-Miranda Associati, Italy
MANUFACTURER
AKABA
CLIENT
AKABA

PRODUCT
Desk
DESIGNER
Fred Baier
FIRM
Fred Baier & Tim Wells
MANUFACTURER
Tim Wells
CLIENT
David Blackburn
PHOTO:
Phil Grey

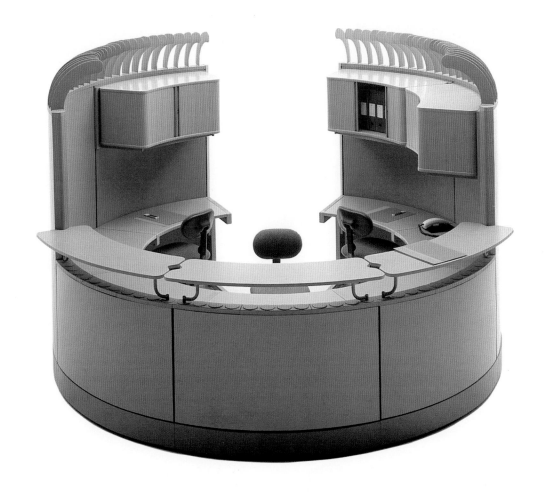

PRODUCT
Space
DESIGNERS
Isao Hosoe, Donato Greco, Ann
Marinelli
FIRM
Isao Hosoe Design, Milan
MANUFACTURER
SACEA, Legnano-Italy
CLIENT
SACEA

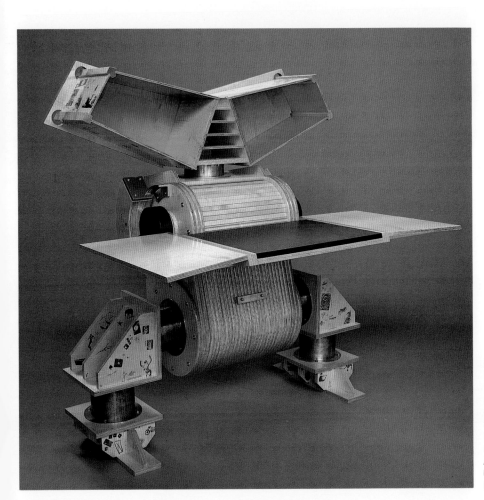

PRODUCT
Dual Quad, Drop Leaf, Roll Top,
Transformer Robot Desk
DESIGNER
Fred Baier
FIRM
Freed Baier & Tim Wells
MANUFACTURER
Arch 18, London
PHOTO
Karen Norquay

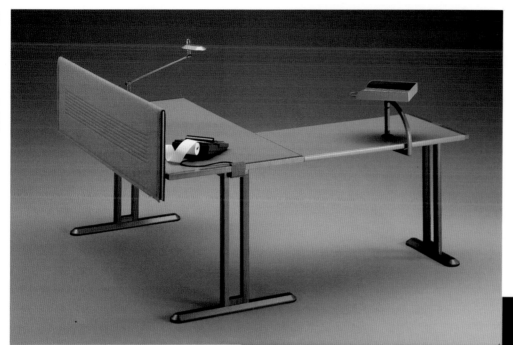

PRODUCT
Zelig Desks
DESIGNER
Giovanni Carino
FIRM
Marcatre' SPA
MANUFACTURER
Marcatre' SPA, Milan

PRODUCT
AnthroBench
DESIGNER
Sohrab Vossoughi
FIRM
Ziba Design
MANUFACTURER
Anthro Corporation
CLIENT
Anthro Corporation

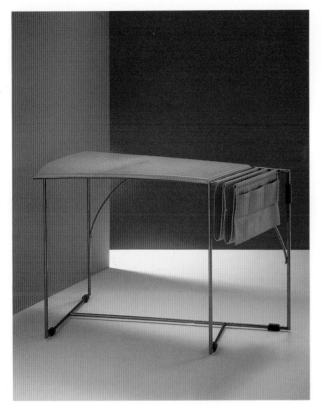

PRODUCT
Tabor Table
DESIGNER
Oscar Tusquets Blanca
MANUFACTURER
Matteo Grassi

PRODUCT
Basys Chair
DESIGNER
Hollington Associates
FIRM
Hollington Associates
MANUFACTURER
Syba Limited UK
CLIENT
Syba Limited UK

PRODUCT
''Akrotiri'' TAble
DESIGNER
Norman Campbell
MANUFACTURER
Art et Industrie/Norman Campbell

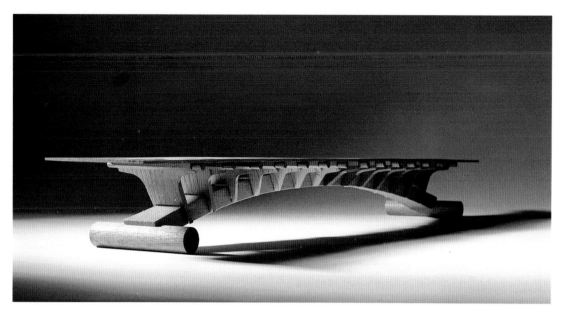

PRODUCT
Table
DESIGNER
Fred Baier
MANUFACTURER
Fred Baier
PHOTOGRAPHER
Karen Norquay

PRODUCT
Tria Table
DESIGNER
Gianfranco Frattini
FIRM
Morphos/Acerbis International
S.P.A.

PRODUCT
Yucatan Coffee Table
FIRM
Neophile
MANUFACTURER
Neophile
CLIENT
Neophile

PRODUCT
Button-edge Hall Table
DESIGNER
Rick Wrigley
FIRM
R.P. Wrigley & Co.
MANUFACTURER
R.P. Wrigley & Co.

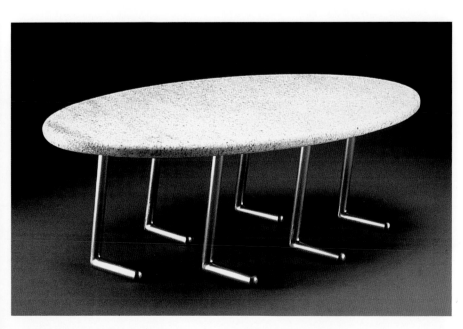

PRODUCT
Coffee Table #3
DESIGNER
Jonathan Bonner

PRODUCT
Kiwara Table
FIRM
Haigh Space
MANUFACTURER
Conde House
AWARDS
1988 ID Design Review Selection,
East Meets West Design Competition
Selection

PRODUCT
Mirage Console Table
DESIGNER
Piotr Sierakowski
FIRM
Koch + Lowy Inc.
MANUFACTURER
Koch + Lowy Inc.

PRODUCT
Kiwara Table
FIRM
Haigh Space
MANUFACTURER
Conde House

PRODUCT
Helix Table
DESIGNER
Iris DeMauro
FIRM
Geo International
MANUFACTURER
Geo International

PRODUCT
"Serenissimo" Table
DESIGNERS
Lella and Massimo Vignelli, David Law
FIRM
Vignelli Designs
MANUFACTURER
Acerbis International
CLIENT
Acerbis International
AWARD
1987 ID Design Review

PRODUCT
Hashi High Table
DESIGNER
Robert Sonneman
FIRM
Sonneman Design Group Inc.
MANUFACTURER
Brueton Industries, Inc.
AWARD
Corporate Design & Realty Award

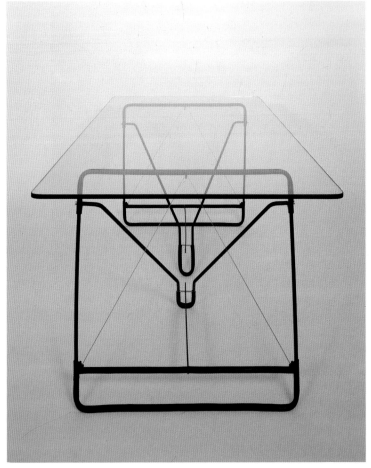

PRODUCT:
Subeybaja Adjustable Table
DESIGNERS:
Robert Heritage, Roger Webb
CLIENT:
See, Ltd.
DESCRIPTION:
Adjustable to cocktail or dining
height

PRODUCT:
''Dipode'' Foldable Table Bases
DESIGNER:
E. Franch
CLIENT:
See, Ltd.

PRODUCT
''Mesa'' Table
DESIGNERS
Roberto Marcatti, Marco Grillo
FIRM
Lavori In Corso
MANUFACTURER
Steel Line

PRODUCT
Post and Ball Table
DESIGNER
Stanley Jay Friedman
FIRM
Stanley Jay Friedman, Inc.
MANUFACTURER
Brueton Industries, Inc.
PHOTO:
Bruce Pollock

PRODUCT
Village Table
DESIGNER
Peter Pierobon
FIRM
Snyderman Gallery
MANUFACTURER
Snyderman Gallery
CLIENT
Private Collection

PRODUCT
Terrible Table
DESIGNER
Michele Oka Doner
FIRM
Art Et Industrie

PRODUCT:
SOLONE Conference Table
DESIGNERS:
Achille Castiglioni
FIRM:
Marcatre' SPA, Italy
MANUFACTURER:
Marcatre' SPA

PRODUCT
Shift Table
DESIGNER
Ettore Sottsass
FIRM
Sottsass Associati
MANUFACTURER
Knoll International

PRODUCT
Two Person Conference Desk
DESIGNER
Sarah Brezavar
FIRM
Brezavar & Brezavar, Architects
MANUFACTURER
W.P.C.

PRODUCT
Shield Vanity Table
DESIGNER
Babette Holland
FIRM
(for) Furniture of the Twentieth
Century
MANUFACTURER
Babette Holland

PRODUCT:
Program ''Indoor''
DESIGNER:
Josep Llusca
FIRM:
Sellex
MANUFACTURER:
Andres Munoz

PRODUCT
"Oasis" Reception Furniture
DESIGNER
Josep Joan Teruel i Samso
FIRM
Blau Comercial S.A., Spain
MANUFACTURER
Josep M. Coma

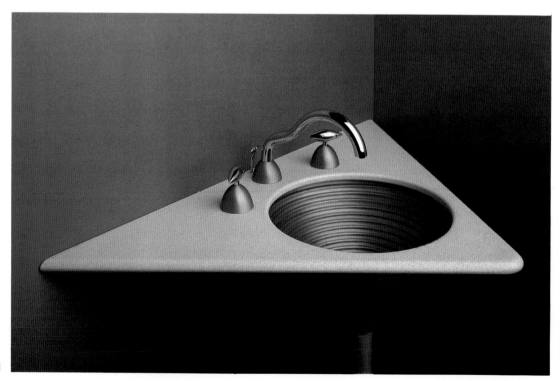

PRODUCT
"Synch"
DESIGNER
Tess Clairmont
PHOTOGRAPHERS
Beth Ludwig, Peter Reitzfeld

PRODUCT
"Starck" Washmobil
DESIGNER
Phillipe Starck
MANUFACTURER
Raspel
CLIENT
Hastings Tile & Il Bagno Collection

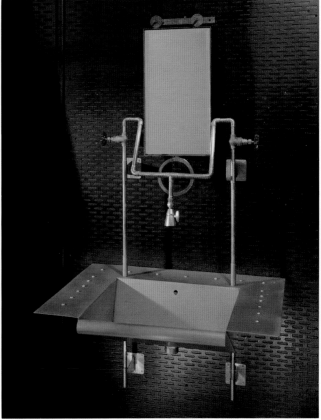

PRODUCT
Bathroom Washbasin
DESIGNER
David Zelman
CLIENT
Hastings Tile & Il Bagno Collection
MANUFACTURER
Prologue 2000 Inc.

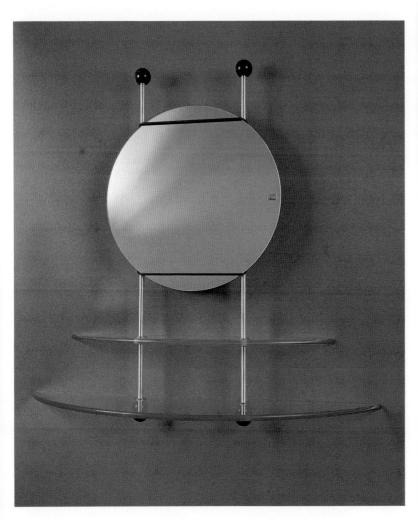

PRODUCT
Mirror
DESIGNER
Emiel Vaasen
FIRM
Duo Design, The Netherlands
MANUFACTURER
Duo Design
CLIENT
Kikkerland Co.

PRODUCT:
Gould's Screen
DESIGNER:
Danny Lane
FIRM:
The Glass Works
MANUFACTURER:
The Glass Works, London
CLIENT:
Dr. and Mrs. Gould private London
residence

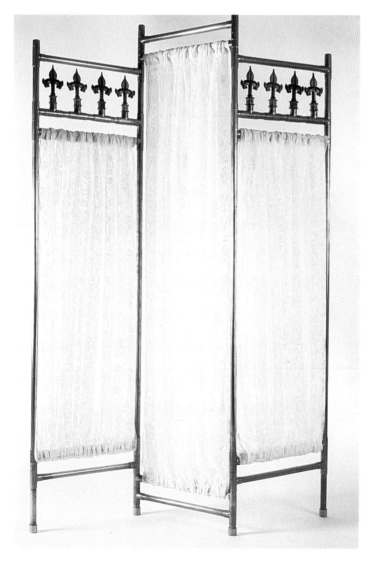

PRODUCT:
Grail Folding Screen
DESIGNER:
Babbette Holland
CLIENT:
Furniture of the 20th Century
MANUFACTURER:
Babbette Holland

PRODUCT:
''Truth Screen''
DESIGNER:
Dan Friedman
CLIENT:
Art et Industrie
MANUFACTURER:
Art et Industrie/Dan Friedman

PRODUCT
Firewood Holder
DESIGNER
Jonathan Bonner

PRODUCT:
''Moonlisteners'' Cabinets
DESIGNER:
Richard Snyder
MANUFACTURER:
Art et Industrie/Richard Snyder

PRODUCT
Brutus Catch-All
DESIGNER
Alexander Polakov
FIRM
Dogworks

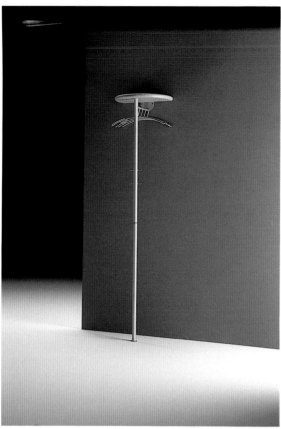

PRODUCT:
"Mur" Clothes Hangers
DESIGNERS:
Gemra Bernal, Ramon Isern
FIRM:
Bernal/Isern
MANUFACTURER:
Grupot, Spain
CLIENT:
Grupot

PRODUCT:
Tea Cart or Auxiliary Cart
DESIGNER:
Jordi Vilanova
FIRM:
Jordi Vilanova, S.A.
MANUFACTURER:
Jordi Vilanova, S.A.

PRODUCT:
"Lucy" Towel Rail With Soap Dish,
Cotton Box, and Tooth Brush Holder
DESIGNERS:
Davide Mercatali, Paolo Pedrizzetti
MANUFACTURER:
Metalplastica Lucchese S.P.A., Italy
CLIENT:
Metalplastica Lucchese S.P.A.

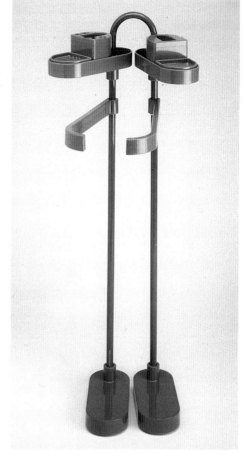

PRODUCT:
Saracino
DESIGNER:
Roberto Marcatti
FIRM:
Lavori In Corso
MANUFACTURER:
Lavori In Corso, Italy

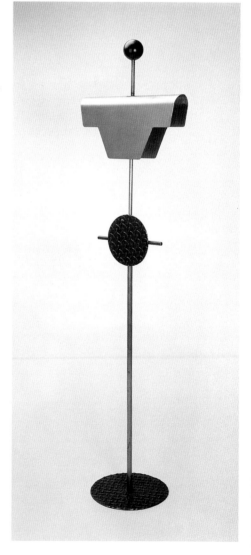

PRODUCT
Easel
DESIGNER
Gregory Glebe
FIRM
Xylem Design

PRODUCT
Night Gallant ''GIGOLO''
DESIGNER
Josep Llusca
FIRM
Enea
MANUFACTURER
Inaki Arzak

PRODUCT
Music Stand
DESIGNER
Fred Baier
MANUFACTURER
Tony Driver
CLIENT
Suzanna Knox
PHOTOGRAPHER
Phil Grey

PRODUCT:
MacGee Shelving Unit
DESIGNER:
Philippe Starck
CLIENT:
See, Ltd.

PRODUCT:
''Howard'' Bookcase
DESIGNER:
Philippe Starck
CLIENT:
Aleph

PRODUCT
Wall Unit
DESIGNER
Shigeru Uchida
FIRM
Studio 80
MANUFACTURER
BUILD Co., Ltd.
CLIENT
Gallery 91
PHOTOGRAPHER
T. Nacasa & Partners
AWARD:
1987 ID Design Review, Selection
PHOTO:
T. Nacasa & Partners

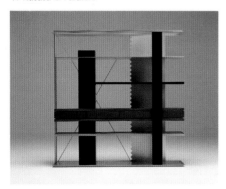

PRODUCT:
''Eliptic'' Cocktail Cabinet
DESIGNER:
Jaime Tresserra Clapes
FIRM:
J. Tresserra Design
MANUFACTURER:
J. Tresserra Design
CLIENT:
J. Tresserra Design
AWARD:
1987 International Furniture Fair,
Valencia

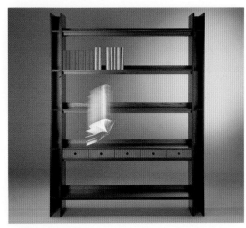

PRODUCT
Libreria Proust
DESIGNER
Gianfranco Frattini
FIRM
MORPHOS (Acerbis International
Division)
MANUFACTURER
MORPHOS
AWARD:
1988 ID Design Review Selection

PRODUCT:
''Max'' Bo
DESIGNERS:
Marco Zanini, Aldo Cibic, Ettore
Sottsass
MANUFACTURER:
Memphis
CLIENT:
Memphis, Milan

PRODUCT:
The Real Wall Clock
DESIGNERS:
Steven Holt, Thomas S. Bley
FIRM:
Zebra Design
MANUFACTURER:
Zelco Industries, Inc.
CLIENT:
Zelco Industries, Inc.

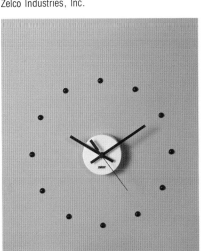

PRODUCT
Monticello Clock Collection
DESIGNER
Piotr Sierakowski
DESIGN FIRM
Koch + Lowy Inc.
Piotr Sierakowski
AWARD:
1988 ID Design Review Honorable
Mention

PRODUCT
Klock Tower
DESIGNERS
Mark Anderson
FIRM
Mark Anderson Design
MANUFACTURER:
One Of A Kind, Ltd.
CLIENT:
One Of A Kind

PRODUCT
''Rack Of Lamb'' etagere
DESIGNER
Terence Main
MANUFACTURER
Art et Industrie/Terence Main

PRODUCT
Q559 Mantel Clock
DESIGNER
Paul Rowan
FIRM
UMBRA U.S.A. Inc.
MANUFACTURER
UMBRA U.S.A. Ltd.

PRODUCT
Philips Wall Clock
DESIGN FIRM
Philips Corporate Industrial Design
CLIENT
Philips

PRODUCT
03 ''Mantel Clock''
DESIGNER
Michael Graves
MANUFACTURER
Alessi, Italy

PRODUCT
Alessi Cuckoo Clock
DESIGNER
Robert Venturi
MANUFACTURER
Alessi, Italy

PRODUCT
Braun Reflex Control AB 50 rsl
DESIGNER
D. Lubs
MANUFACTURER
Braun AG, W. Germany
CLIENT
Braun, Inc.
DESCRIPTION
Wave hand in front of clock face
and alarm stops.

PRODUCT
Spring Clock – ATC35 by Artimor
FIRM
Canetti Inc.
MANUFACTURER
Collector's Collection
CLIENT
Canetti Inc.

PRODUCT
Halo Clock
DESIGNER
Kazuo Kawasaki
CLIENT
Gallery 91
PHOTOGRAPHER
Masao Ueda

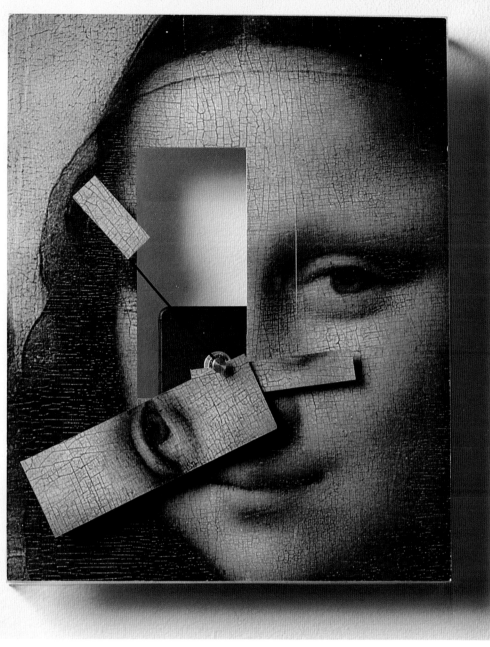

PRODUCT:
Deconstruction Clock ''Monalisa''
DESIGNER:
Constantin Boym
FIRM:
Red Square
CLIENT::
Gallery 91
AWARD:
1988 ID Design Review Honorable
Mention

PRODUCT
Philips Alarm Clock
DESIGN FIRM
Philips Corporate Industrial Design
CLIENT
Philips

Andrée Putman
President
Studio Ecart

Whether it is textiles, tabletop objects or mannequins, I approach everything instinctually and personally—in a way that has little to do with technique or ideas. Some people work very well with ideas, but I work better with visions and dreams that have been transported like luggage from my childhood. They aren't as easy to articulate.

I also work with a sense of humor. I once did a rug which looked like ribbons spread on the floor. And the ribbons became a theme. Maybe it's an idea, but it's not an intellectual one. When I read what all these great designers say about design, I admire them, but they are so talkative about their thinking. For me, when something works, it always comes from being sincere and from deep inside.

•

When I look at an object, I look to see if it has a past, a subtext that extends beyond the object. I have an enormous respect for things that are timeless. Some things cross time with enormous grace; they have this mysterious, eternal beauty. And usually they are very simple. I also respect things that are classics — very sophisticated and far from the danger of being dated. With things that appear not to have been inspired by anything that came before, you get the feeling of absolute innovation. I believe that people are obsessed with modernity, but often they confuse modern with contemporary. To me, modernity doesn't only mean "today." It is something completely mysterious that has nothing to do with the future or any foreshadowing of the future. Instead, it involves things that pass through time easily, that don't have ups and downs with trends. Some Egyptian things are 4,000 years old and amazingly modern.

That notion of modernity applies to everything in design. I'm a fan of (stage director) Robert Wilson and I realized that the first plays I saw of his had more to do with eternity than with modernity, though they are thoroughly modern. And although

I cannot quote him, the poet Baudelaire once said that modernity doesn't negate the past; it negates the present in which things seem to be eternally repeated.

•

I took another path to design, via music, and the two disciplines relate very much. I was about to become a composer and after having dedicated my first 21 years to music, a famous musician told me that I had to spend 10 more years in a room with paper and erasers...I couldn't face it.

I didn't go right into design, but instead developed by doing small jobs. I soon realized my ideas were kind of revolutionary. From my 20s until 10 years ago, I was viewed as someone who was totally marginal, who had no focus. But I didn't mind. I was absorbing everything—the best of today—and since I had some knowledge of the past and my parents were also somewhat eccentric, I didn't feel unhappy or bitter about having a career that was nothing and many things at the same time.

The difference between fashion and style is that fashion is so fragile it's almost touching. It's very short, like certain insects who, I'm told, die only a few hours after they are born. Style, on the other hand, endures.

Clothes don't have meaning any more, especially in America. They don't announce who you are. There used to be all these very depressing distinctions, like if you wore couture, it meant you were rich. This has totally disappeared. People with style will wear a t-shirt from Lamston's with an Armani jacket and maybe a sailor's bag instead of a purse. They aren't addicted to designers who dictate what they wear.

I had an aunt who I remember saying, "Oh, I just dread having to wear long red skirts this year." This concept doesn't exist anymore. Fashion is like champagne—it's not changing people's lives.

Today, there are no more fashion victims, just design victims, because today people

express more through design than clothes. And this is becoming very dangerous for designers who license their names to all sorts of products. I needn't say more.

•

Most designers think they invent things. Not me. I'm more modest. People like Eileen Gray or Pierre Charrot or Frank Gehry were and are real inventors because they changed the way one could think about designing a hanger, or a table or a house.

Instead, my strength is my personal sensitivity blended with a lot of eclecticism; the ability to reconcile things that are apparent contradictions. I have found that I can make objects that do not age by combining things that don't necessarily belong together but create an ensemble. It's funny because people have called me daring. But I'm not. I still work very intensely with more and more doubt about what I do. I don't have a triumphant attitude, and I am not a saint and I think people realize it.

To me, the best thing about America is that people know me in the streets. Not the dignified people—they don't talk to me— but occasionally messengers come up to me on the street and say, "Hey, Miss Putman, how ya' doin'." To be honest, my greatest reward is to have been an influence on that part of that world. My generation doesn't understand what I do.

PRODUCT
''Slate'' Fabric
DESIGNERS
Pina Manzone, Howard Friedman,
Al Salsano
FIRM
Scalamanndre
MANUFACTURER
Scalamanndre
CLIENT
Scalamanndre

PRODUCT
"Indian Summer," "Harvest,"
"Allspice" Tweeds
FIRM
Etalage Fabrics/Wallcoverings Inc.

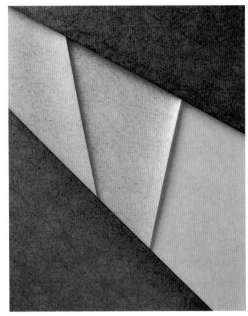

PRODUCT
"Tracery" Wallcovering
DESIGNER
Maya Romanoff
FIRM
Maya Romanoff, Inc.
MANUFACTURER
Maya Romanoff, Inc.

PRODUCT
Wilshire Panel Fabric
DESIGNER
Mark N. Smith
FIRM
Steelcase Inc.
MANUFACTURER
Steelcase Inc.
AWARD:
I.B.D. Product Award

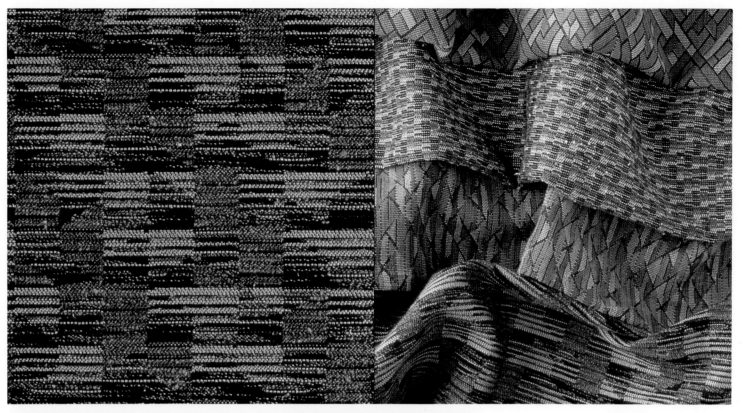

PRODUCT
Jhane Barnes Designs for Knoll
DESIGNER
Jhane Barnes
FIRM
Jhane Barnes
MANUFACTURER
Knoll International
CLIENT
Knoll International
PHOTO:
Rick Muller

PRODUCT
''Chicago'' Fabric
DESIGNER:
Andree Putman
MANUFACTURER:
Romanex de Boussac

PRODUCT
Scarves
DESIGNER
Junichi Arai
FIRM
Eastern Accent
MANUFACTURER
Nuno
CLIENT
Nuno

PRODUCT
Scarves
DESIGNER
Junichi Arai
FIRM
Eastern Accent
MANUFACTURER
Nuno
CLIENT
Nuno

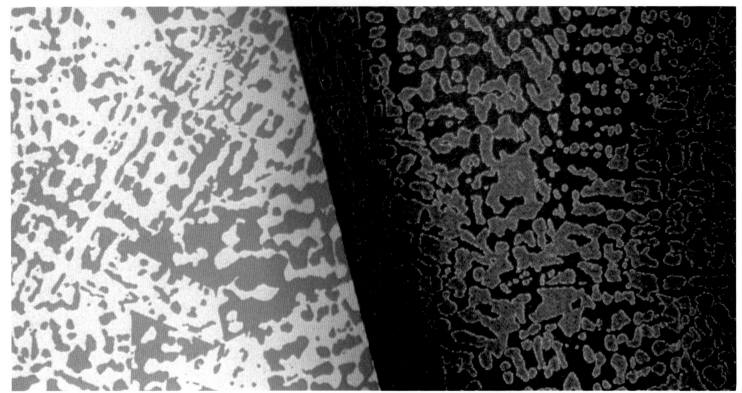

PRODUCT
Scarves
DESIGNER
Junichi Arai
FIRM
Eastern Accent
MANUFACTURER
Nuno
CLIENT
Nuno

PRODUCT
''Arras'' Woven Tapestry
DESIGNER
Glenn Peckman
FIRM
Donghia Textiles
MANUFACTURER
Donghia Textiles

PRODUCT
''Lille'' Woven Textile
DESIGNER
Donghia Design Studio
FIRM
Donghia Textiles
MANUFACTURER
Donghia Textiles

PRODUCT
''Trace'' Fabric
DESIGNER
Andree Putman
MANUFACTURER
Romanex de Boussac

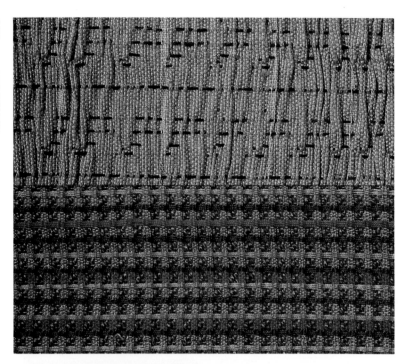

PRODUCT
Y.P. Woven Textiles
DESIGNER
Andrea Stix Wasserman
FIRM
Andrea Stix Wasserman
MANUFACTURER
Omori Textiles (scarf), Japan,
Andrea Stix Wasserman (large
weavings)

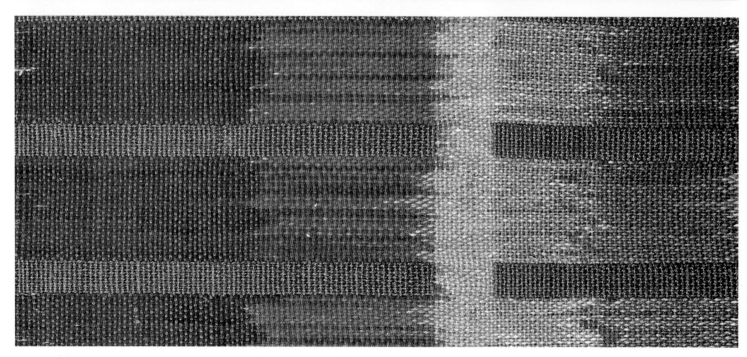

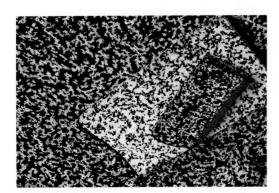

PRODUCT
''Composition Collection'' Towels
DESIGNER
Eternal
FIRM
Eastern Accent
CLIENT
Eternal

PRODUCT
''Graniti'' Wallcovering
DESIGNER
Donghia Design Studio
FIRM
Donghia Textiles
MANUFACTURER
Donghia Textiles
AWARDS
1987 I.B.D., 1987 ROSCOE

PRODUCT
''Salina'' Wallcovering
DESIGNERS
Gary and Carrie Golkin
FIRM
Art People
MANUFACTURER
Art People

PRODUCT
Roadway Tablecloth, Paris Map
Napkin, Tire Napkin Ring
DESIGNER
Zelda Linnon
FIRM
Chateau X

PRODUCT
Plastic Coated Cotton Print
Tablecloth, Placemat With Ball
Fringe, Coasters With Ball Fringe
DESIGNER
Zelda Linnon
FIRM
Chateau X

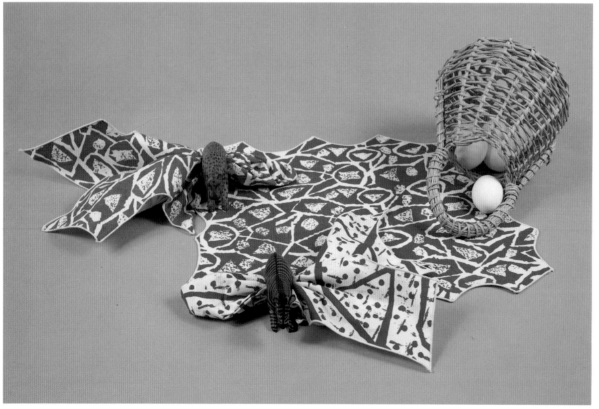

PRODUCT
''Temmi'' and ''Abijahn'' Table
Skins
DESIGNER
Kerris Wolsky
FIRM
Harlem Textile Works/ Children's
Art Carnival
MANUFACTURER
Harlem Textile Works/ Children's
Art Carnival

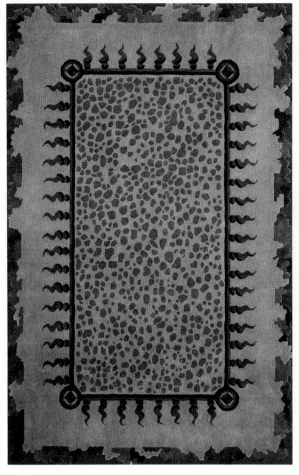

PRODUCT
''Urban Garden #1''
DESIGNER
Robert Gaul
FIRM
Archetype GalleryGEO International
MANUFACTURER
GEO International

PRODUCT
Rug
DESIGNER
Andree Putman
MANUFACTURER
Toulemonde Bochart

PRODUCT
''Fire In The Lake'' Area Rug
DESIGNERS
Carolyn and Vincent Carleton
FIRM
Carleton Designs
MANUFACTURER
Carleton Designs
CLIENT
Panarace/Remitz Residence
AWARD
1987 ROSCOE, Best Contemporary
Rug Design

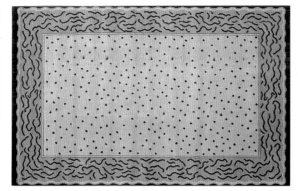

PRODUCT
Rug
DESIGNER
Andree Putman
MANUFACTURER
Toulemonde Bochart

PRODUCT
Maison Carree
DESIGNERS
Luca Scacchetti
FIRM
Sisal Collezioni

PRODUCT
''Mare'' and ''Terra''
DESIGNER
Daniela Puppa
FIRM
Sisal Collezioni

Sisal Collezsioni

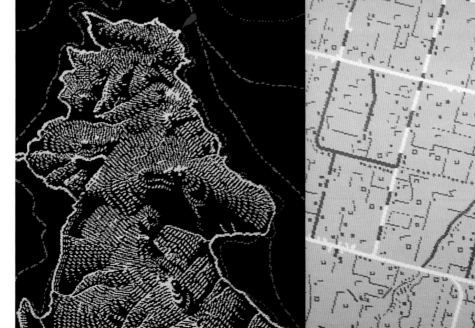

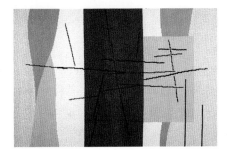

PRODUCT
Agadir
DESIGNER
Luca Scacchetti
FIRM
Sisal Collezioni

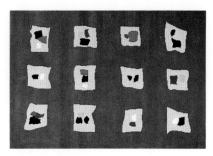

PRODUCT
I Problemi Sul Tappeto
DESIGNER
Bruno Munari
FIRM
Sisai Collezsioni

Sisal Collezioni

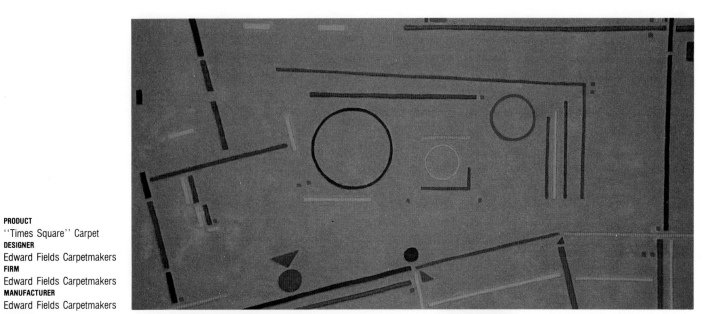

PRODUCT
''Times Square'' Carpet
DESIGNER
Edward Fields Carpetmakers
FIRM
Edward Fields Carpetmakers
MANUFACTURER
Edward Fields Carpetmakers

PRODUCT
''Tooth and Nail'' Handscreened
Border
DESIGNER
Ken Cornet
FIRM
Ken Cornet
MANUFACTURER
A. Musticorn & Co.

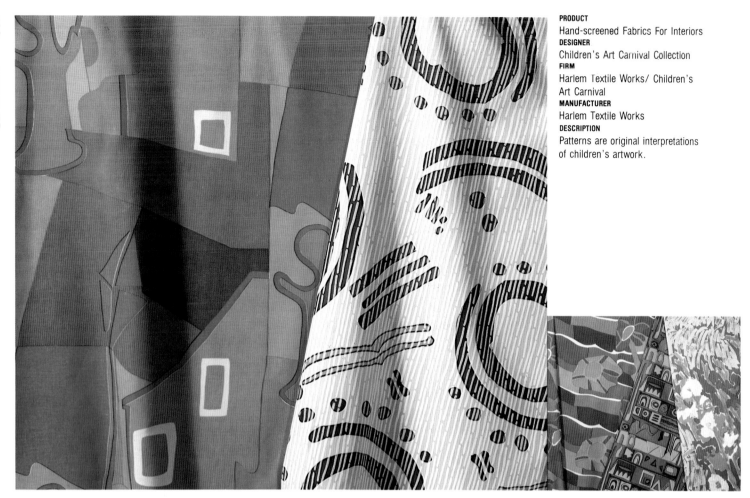

PRODUCT
Hand-screened Fabrics For Interiors
DESIGNER
Children's Art Carnival Collection
FIRM
Harlem Textile Works/ Children's
Art Carnival
MANUFACTURER
Harlem Textile Works
DESCRIPTION
Patterns are original interpretations
of children's artwork.

PRODUCT
''Cedit'' Tiles
DESIGNERS
Ettore Sottsass, Marco Zanini
FIRM
Sottsass Associati
MANUFACTURER
Cedit
PHOTO
Aldo Ballo

PRODUCT
''Asterix'' Tiles
DESIGNER
Dorothy Hafner

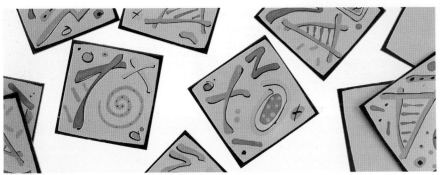

PRODUCT
''Heavy Texture'' Wallcovering
DESIGNERS
Gary and Carrie Golkin
FIRM
Art People
MANUFACTURER
Art People

PRODUCT
''Rathbone'' Wallcovering
DESIGNERS
Gary and Carrie Golkin
FIRM
Art People
MANUFACTURER
Art People

CHAPTER 5

EQUIPMENT

Hartmut Esslinger
President
frogdesign

"Good design" is always hard to define. I compare it to good nutrition—when you begin to eat well, you don't realize it at first. But as soon as you begin to feel better, you can't go back to eating bad food.

No matter the product, there are four components to any "good design":
—Strategy. A company must have a strategic advantage that keeps it ahead of everything in the market. For example, Sony has Trinitron. Enough said.
—Quality. If there is no quality, a product can never be good. If the manufacturer makes junk, get out of your relationship with him or her.
—Innovation. A product must be something new that people really need, whether it fills a gap in the market or whether it serves society as a whole. Often companies try to avoid progress. Fight them.
—Aesthetics. If you look at design as art, it must be beautiful. But if a product is only beautiful and nothing else, it's not design.

•

Craftsmanship hasn't suffered as a result of industrialization— it has been out for a long, long time. In the age of industrial production, craftsmanship is an obstacle. One hundred years ago, a man might have produced 2,000 chairs in a year. Today, a company produces 2 million. What's important today is manu-facturability. But there are other considerations, like the environment. Using chrome in production is terrible because it destroys the environment. At frogdesign, we refuse to use it as well as other harmful materials like asbestos, PVC or fiberglass. We started one office furniture company in Germany that was ecologically safe because we think this is an issue that must be addressed.

•

Designers aren't the inventors of our time. We are the artists of our time. For a long time, archi-tecture dominated; then it was film, then video and electronic media. The next and last art—

so far—has been design. That means being able to produce and multiply a product in millions that is still beautiful. Without the art, design is just dead engineering.

But then you must ask, what is art? I think art is something you cannot choose; instead, it chooses you. At first I tried a professional sports career. That didn't work, so I tried to be a rock 'n roll musician. That didn't work so I joined the Army. Then I tried electronic engineering, but after five months I quit. I realized that I shouldn't have been an engineer. I discovered design and knew that was what I should do. I didn't have a choice anymore.

•

As an engineer you can have books and formulas. As a designer, you're naked out in the world. If you're not good, every-one sees it. In that way, it's a very honest profession.

I approach design very person-ally: If I do a product, I want to be able to bring it home. If I'm ashamed of it, I won't do it. You must have a personal identity in the product. If we get a project at frog and no one is able to identify with it, we cannot do it.

I think experimentation is critically important. So is using color. Today for example, I have on red socks, orange shoelaces, and a shirt with 50 colors in it. I protest the lack of color. That is one of many drawbacks with big production. Another is the bad taste that has become the necessary evil of big volume. As a result, you settle on black, light grey or beige. For some reason, America has also settled on woodgrain.

•

In the '60s we recovered freedom in design and everyone was filled with idealism. In the '70s we had to cope with austerity: energy was in short supply and we started feeling the manipulations of big corpora-tions. As a result, we had to make more with less. We learned that everything has its limits and the challenge became to make something better within those limits. That's why I think the Japanese are doing so well today

—they are used to limitations.

In the '90s, my dream is that we will be able to use technology to serve more people. We will **also** have to open new opportunities for more emotional designs because other freedoms may be more constricted. Take driving as an example. Using your car at the wrong time of day on a crowded freeway makes it impossible to feel the freedom associated with driving. In the future it will just get worse. As a result, design should get more emotional, more tranquil and enjoyable because how we do things will be more important than what we do. Design should be more than just hardware—it should be an event or an experience. "Form follows e/motion." We trademarked that phrase last year.

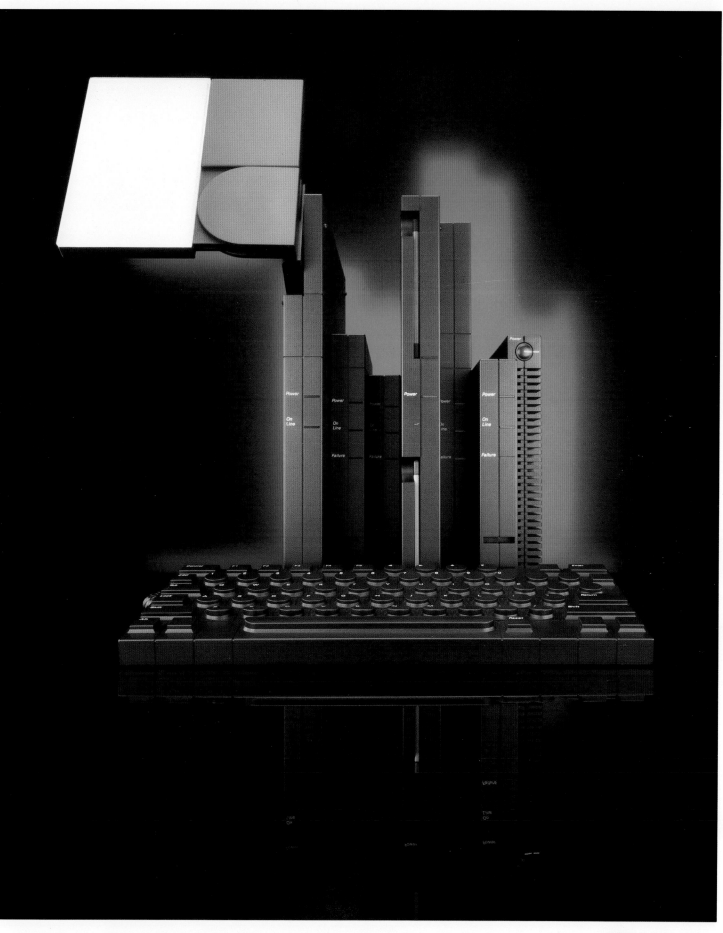

PRODUCT
''Book'' Computer–Concept
DESIGNER
D.M. Gresham
FIRM
Design Logic
CLIENT
Watertechnics

PRODUCT
Conceptual Computer Terminal
FIRM
Design Central
CLIENT
Deutches Arkitectur Museum

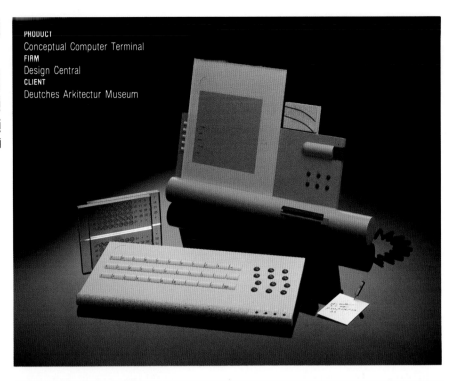

PRODUCT
Scribe
DESIGNERS
David Reichman, Peter Langmar
FIRM
D.R. Design

AWARD
1988 ID Annual Design Review
Selection
DESCRIPTION
Portable file system which records
handwriting on a digitizing pad.

PRODUCT
Experimental Design Personal
Computers
DESIGNERS
Adam Grosser, Gavin Ivester
FIRM
Apple Computer Inc.
PHOTO
John Long
AWARD
1988 Annual Design Review
Selection

PRODUCT
AFI 500 Automated Airline Ticket
Dispenser
DESIGNERS
Sohrab Vossoughi, Bill Daleabout
FIRM
Ziba Design
MANUFACTURER
AFI Technologies, Inc.
CLIENT
AFI Technologies, Inc.
AWARD
1988 IDSA N.W. Design Invitational

PRODUCT
LCD Computer Terminal–concept
DESIGNER
Daniel Wickemeyer
FIRM
Slam Design
AWARD:
1988 ID Annual Design Review
Selection

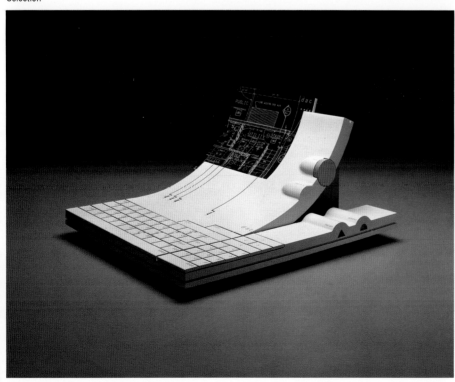

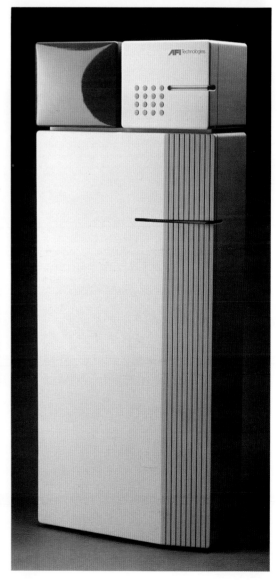

PRODUCT
GRIDLITE Laptop Computer
DESIGNER
Winfried Scheuer
FIRM
ID TWO
AWARDS
Design Innovative '88
1987 ID Annual Design Review

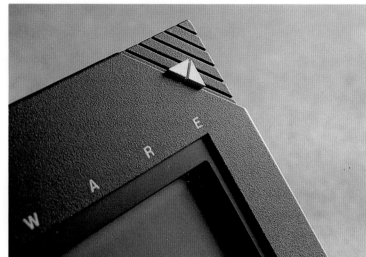

PRODUCT
Touchware PC Translator
DESIGNERS
Robin Chu, Bob Yaun
FIRM
ID TWO
CLIENT
Newex Inc.
AWARDS
1988 Designers & Art Directors'
Association British Product Design
Award; 1987 ID Annual Design
Review

PRODUCT
Conceptual Computer
DESIGNER
Chris Barlow

PRODUCT
Workstation Terminal Design
DESIGNERS
D.M. Gresham, Martin Thaler,
James Ludwig
FIRM
Design Logic
CLIENT
RC Computer a/s

PRODUCT
Knowledge Navigator/2 Display
DESIGNER
Gavin Ivester
FIRM
Apple Computer, Inc.
MANUFACTURER
Apple Computer, Inc.
CLIENT
Apple Computer, Inc.
PHOTOGRAPHER
Rick English

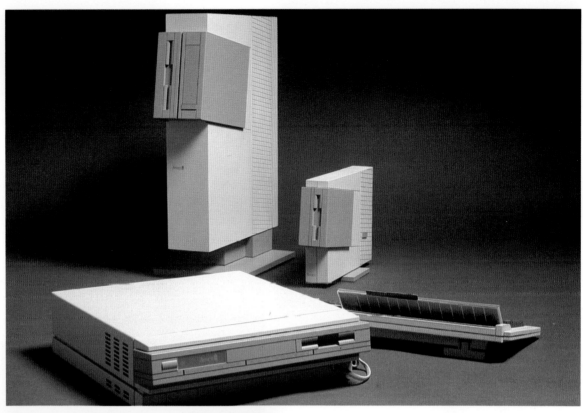

PRODUCT
Archimedes Microcomputer
DESIGNERS
John Stoddard, Nick Dormon, Marc Tanner
FIRM
Moggridge Associates
CLIENT
Acorn Computers, UK

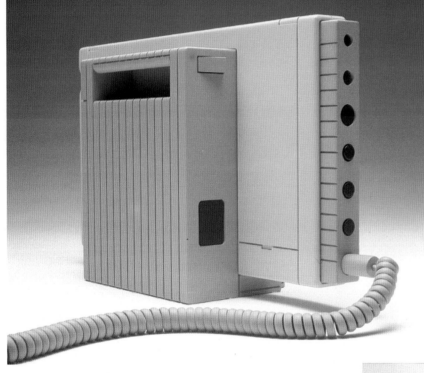

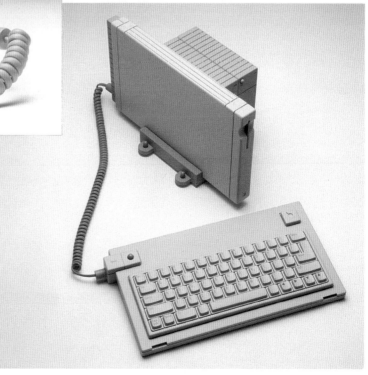

PRODUCT
Advanced Transportable Computer Concept
DESIGNERS
Robert Brunner, Ken Wood
FIRM
Lunar Design Incorporated
MANUFACTURER
Apple Computer, Inc.
CLIENT
Apple Computer, Inc.

PRODUCT
Intelligent Telephone
DESIGNER
ninaber/peters/krouwel
MANUFACTURER
PTT-telecommunications
AWARD
1987 Holland In Vorm Exhibition
DESCRIPTION
Telephone with personal computer
chipcard reader.

PRODUCT
Migent MM 1200 ''Pocket Modem''
DESIGNER
Ron Clements
FIRM
Designfour
CLIENT
Migent, Inc.

AWARD
IDSA Industrial Design Excellence
Certificate

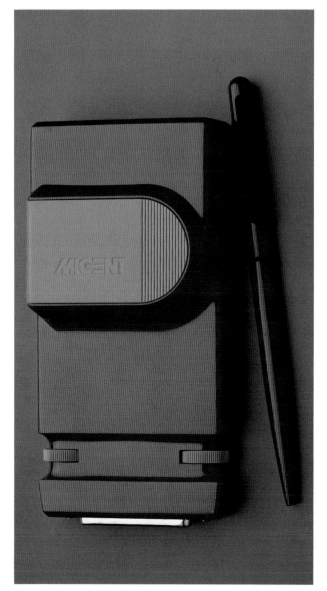

PRODUCT
Cirrus Fast Disk/Tape Back Up
Series
DESIGNER
Sohrab Vossoughi, Jon Bisha
FIRM
Ziba Design
MANUFACTURER
LaCie, Ltd.

DESCRIPTION
Add-on Peripherals for Apple's
Macintosh Plus Systems.

PRODUCT
Cable Connector
DESIGNERS
Gene Yanku, Rich Ragsdale
FIRM
Tandem Computers, Inc.
MANUFACTURER
Tandem Computers, Inc.
CLIENT
Tandem Computers, Inc.

DESCRIPTION
Connector needs no screws. It
simply snaps on and releases by
pushing a button.
AWARD
1987 ''IF''-DIE Gute Industrieform

PRODUCT
Amtel Direct Line Printer
DESIGNER
Jeff Smith
FIRM
Lunar Design Incorporated
MANUFACTURER
Amtel
CLIENT
Amtel
AWARD
1987 ID Annual Design Review
Selection

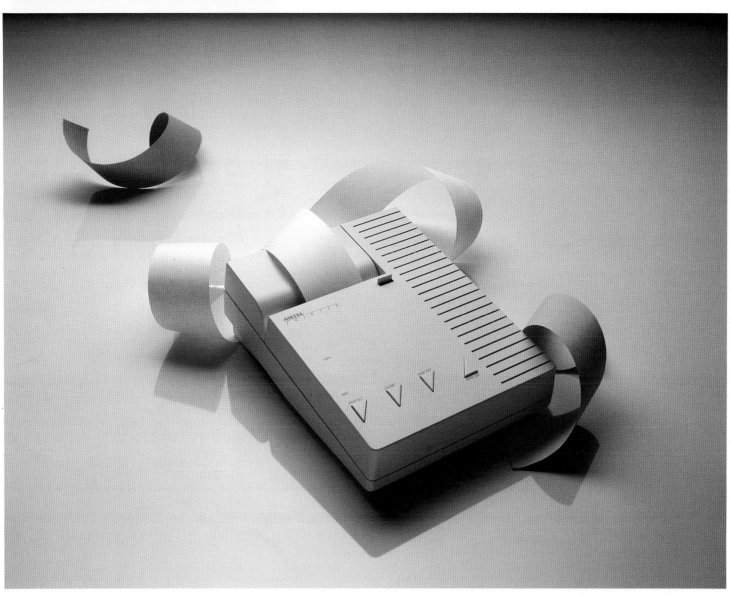

PRODUCT
CUVAX MC50 Hand-Held Copier
DESIGNER
Ricoh Corporation

PRODUCT
Handy Copier Z-HC1
DESIGNER
Information Systems Design Center;
Corporate Design Center
CLIENT
Sharp Corporation

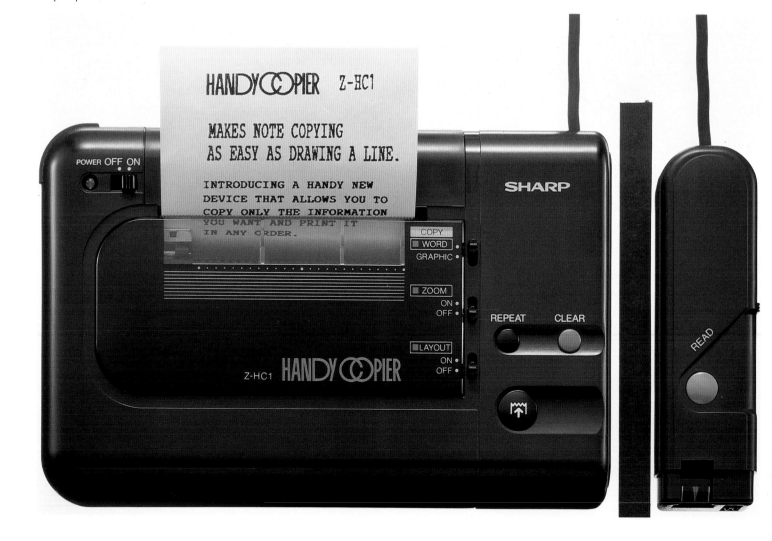

PRODUCT
Digital Personal Copier FN-P300
DESIGNER
Matsushita Electric Industrial Co.,
Ltd.
Office Equipment Dividion
FIRM
Matsushita Electric Industrial Co.,
Ltd.

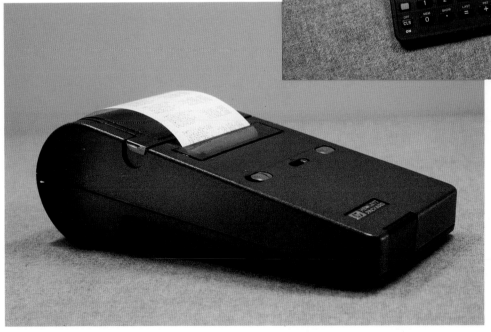

PRODUCT
Portable Infrared Printer
DESIGNER
Gary Podwalny
FIRM
Hewlett-Packard
MANUFACTURER
Hewlett-Packard

PRODUCT
Image Maker
DESIGNERS
Michael Nuttall, Nelson Au
FIRM
Matrix Product Design Inc.
DESIGNERS
Walt Conti, Dennis Boyle
FIRM
David Kelley Design
CLIENT
Presentation Technology
PHOTOGRAPHER
John Long
AWARD
1987 Annual ID Design Review
Selection

PRODUCT
Artograph ''Statmaker'' Statcamera
DESIGNERS:
Dan Cunagin, Michael Krol, Eugene
Reshanov, Lars Runquist
FIRM:
Polivka Logan Designers, Inc.
MANUFACTURER:
Artograph
AWARD:
1988 ID Design Review Selection

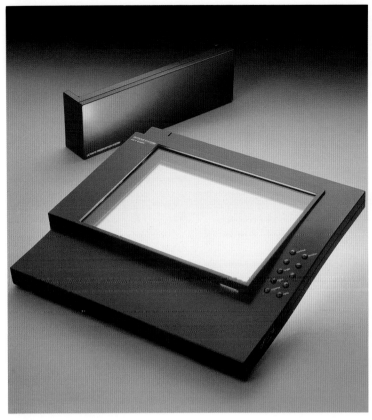

PRODUCT
PC Viewer 6448C/6448C+2
DESIGNERS
Christopher Alviar, Sohrab
Vossoughi
FIRM
Ziba Design
MANUFACTURER
InFocus Systems, Inc.
CLIENT
InFocus Systems, Inc.
AWARD
1988 IDSA N.W. Design Invitational
DESCRIPTION
Electronic overhead transparency
system for personal computers.

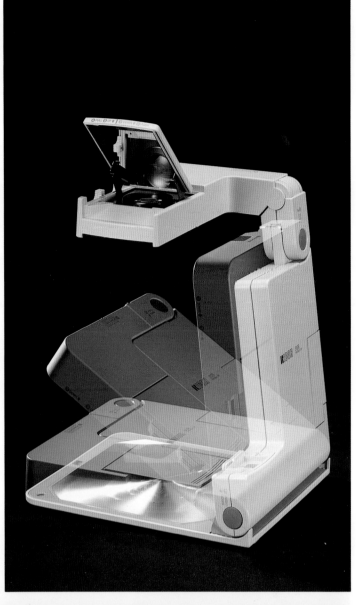

PRODUCT
Portable Copier
FIRM
Ricoh Corporation

PRODUCT
ID 4 Plus Camera
DESIGNERS
Michael Dolan, Eric Chan
FIRM
Chan+Dolan Industrial Design Inc.
MANUFACTURER
Optical & Electronic Research Inc.
CLIENT
Optical & Electronic Research Inc.
DESCRIPTION
Produces 4 instant ID Polaroid
photos per film sheet.

PRODUCT
LaserWriter II Printer
FIRM
Apple Computer, Inc.
MANUFACTURER
Apple Computer, Inc.
CLIENT
Apple Computer, Inc.

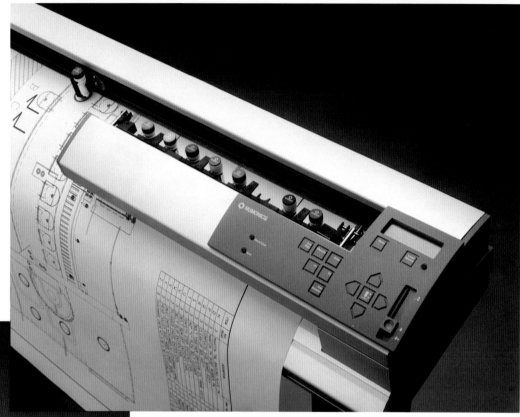

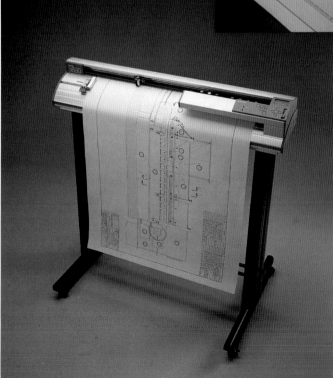

PRODUCT
"E" Size Plotter
DESIGNER
Tom Watters
FIRM
The Design Works
MANUFACTURER
Numonics Corporation
CLIENT
Numonics Corporation

DESCRIPTION
Multi-pen plotter for architectural
and engineering PC based CAD
systems.

PRODUCT
''Elaine'' Office Printer
DESIGNER
Loyd Moore
FIRM
Technology Design

AWARDS
1986 ID Annual Design Review
Selection, 1986 IDEA Award

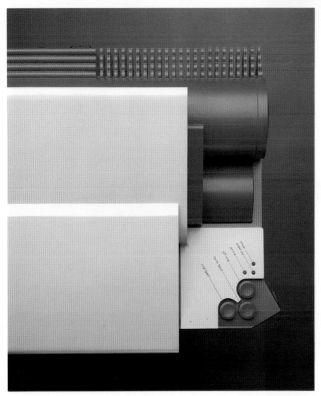

PRODUCT
Trackball Mouse
DESIGNERS
Stephen Peart, Brad Bissell
FIRM
Vent Design Associates
MANUFACTURER
Abaton Technology Inc.
CLIENT
Abaton Technology Inc.

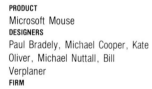

PRODUCT
Microsoft Mouse
DESIGNERS
Paul Bradely, Michael Cooper, Kate Oliver, Michael Nuttall, Bill Verplaner
FIRM
Matrix Product Design Inc.

CLIENT
Microsoft
PHOTO
Rick English
AWARD
1988 ID Annual Design Review Selection

PRODUCT
Fold And Roll Choral Riser
DESIGNERS
Ken Staten, O. David Rogers
FIRM
Stage Right Corporation

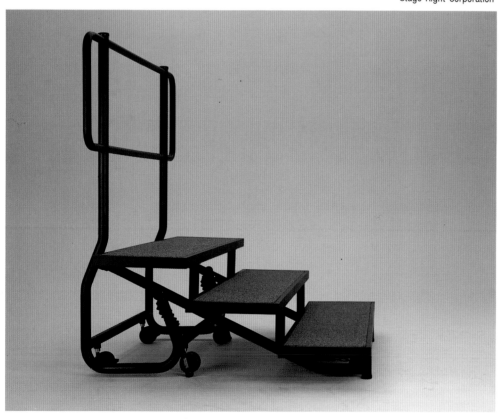

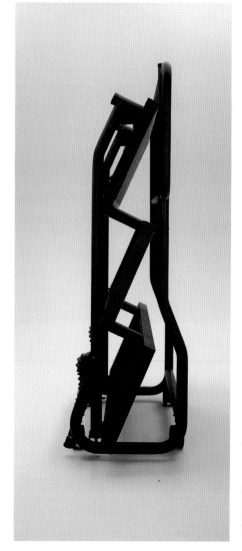

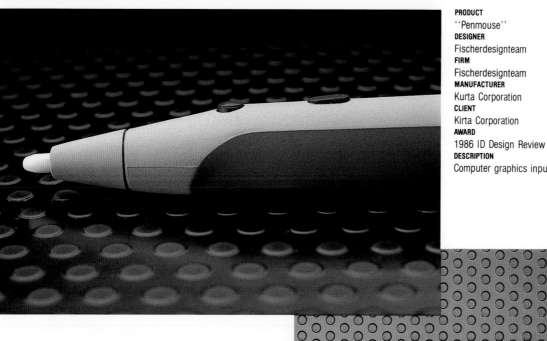

PRODUCT
''Penmouse''
DESIGNER
Fischerdesignteam
FIRM
Fischerdesignteam
MANUFACTURER
Kurta Corporation
CLIENT
Kirta Corporation
AWARD
1986 ID Design Review
DESCRIPTION
Computer graphics input device.

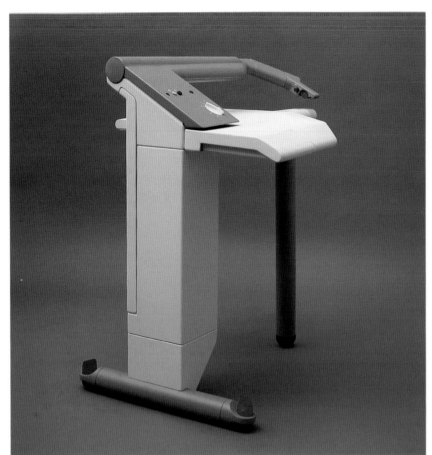

PRODUCT
Semi Industrial Machine For
Assembling Synthetic Textile
DESIGNER
Damien Bihr
FIRM
Naos Industrial Design, Belgium
AWARD
Braun Competition

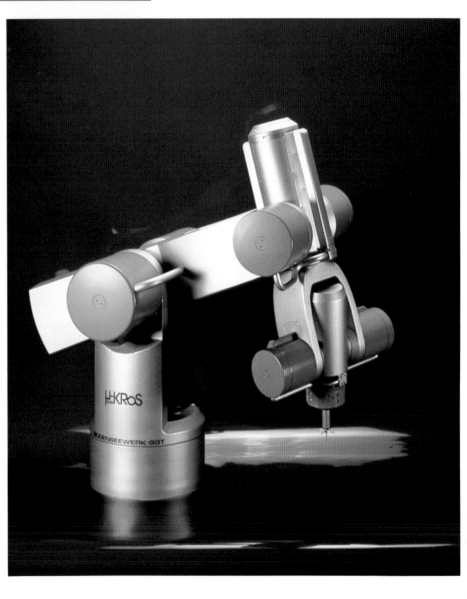

PRODUCT
Robot M-Kronos
DESIGNER
Hartmut Esslinger
FIRM
frogdesign
CLIENT
Bodenseewerke Uberlingen
AWARD
Design Center Stuttgart, ''IF''
Hanover

PRODUCT
Honeywell 4500 Circular Chart
Recorder
DESIGNERS
Eric A. Schneider, John D.
Coleman, G. Gordon Fluke
FIRM
Bresslergroup
MANUFACTURER
Honeywell, Inc.
CLIENT
Honeywell, Inc.
DESCRIPTION
Monitors temperature and other
variables in food manufacturing.

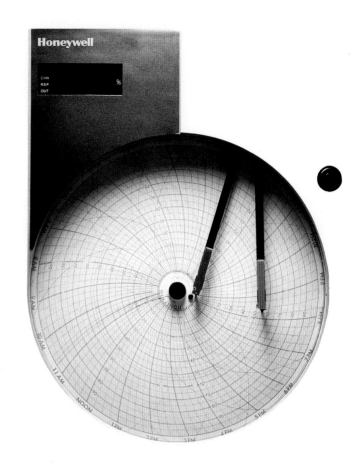

PRODUCT
Ultrasonic Cleaner
DESIGNERS
Bill Bartlett, David Hines, Ed Cruz
FIRM
Bartlett Design Associates, Inc.
MANUFACTURER
Identechs Corporation
CLIENT
Identechs Corporation
DESCRIPTION
Cleans small industrial parts, but
expands double its vertical size for
larger parts.

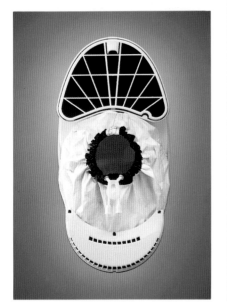

PRODUCT
Pureflo Self Contained Respirators
FIRM
Random Ltd., UK
DESCRIPTION
To use in industry or fume-laden
environments

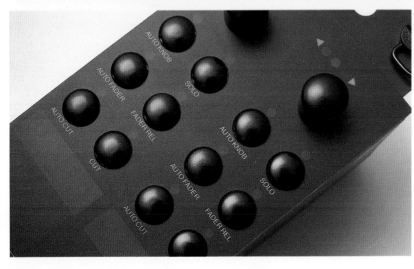

PRODUCT
Edit Droid and Sound Droid Video
and Sound Editing Consoles
DESIGNERS
Robert Brunner, Jeff Smith, Ken
Wood, Gerard Furbershaw
FIRM
The Droid Works
MANUFACTURER
The Droid Works
AWARD
1987 IDSA Recognition Award

PRODUCT
Elgin Premier Whirlwind Street
Sweeper
DESIGNERS
Douglas F. Wolff, William A. Lee,
Charles E. Steele, Steven W.
Erikson
FIRM
KMH Design
MANUFACTURER
Elgin Sweeper Company
CLIENT
Elgin Sweeper Company

PRODUCT
Crown Supercoach Schoolbus
DESIGNERS
Edmund Britt, James MacConkey,
Michael Mercadante, Philip Reavis,
Eric Swartz
FIRM
Loeffler-MacConkey Inc.
CLIENT
Crown Coach, Inc.

PRODUCT
AC Motor
DESIGNER
Hartmut Esslinger
FIRM
frogdesign
CLIENT
General Electric Company
AWARD
1988 ID Design Review Selection

PRODUCT
"Tangara" Double Deck Commuter
Train
DESIGNERS
Michael Groves, Jonathan Sothcott,
Tony Hume
FIRM
DCA Design International Ltd.
MANUFACTURER
Goninan & Co. Ltd., Australia
CLIENT
State Rail Authority of New South
Wales

PRODUCT
Electro-Powered Variable Vehicle
DESIGNER
Angela Knoop
AWARD
1986 Braun Prize

PRODUCT
Driver Guide
DESIGNERS
Nelson Au, Michael Nuttall
FIRM
Matrix Product Design Inc.
DESIGNERS
Mark Glusker, James Yurchenco
FIRM
David Kelley Design
CLIENT
Karlin & Collins
PHOTOGRAPHER
Rick English
AWARD:
1987 ID Design Review Selection
DESCRIPTION:
Prints out directions to desired
location when destination is input.

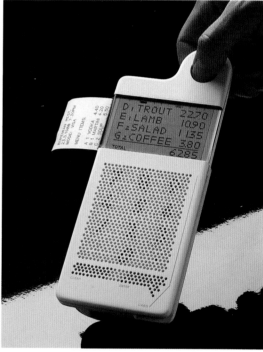

PRODUCT
Transaction Terminal System
DESIGNER
Vlad Muller, M.A.
FIRM
Muller/Ullmann Industrial
Designers, Canada
CLIENT
Muller/Ullmann Industrial Designers

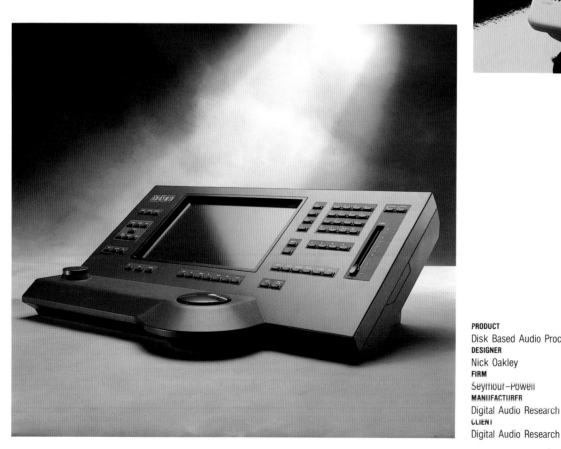

PRODUCT
Disk Based Audio Processor Console
DESIGNER
Nick Oakley
FIRM
Seymour-Powell
MANUFACTURER
Digital Audio Research
CLIENT
Digital Audio Research

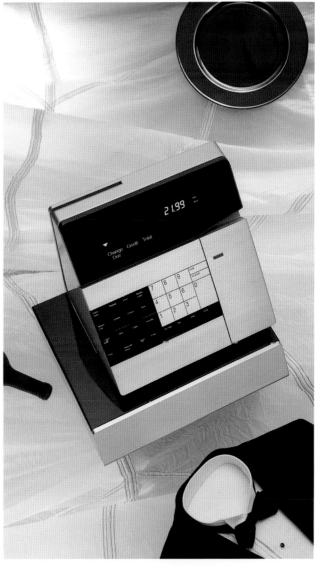

PRODUCT
Conceptual Electronic Cash Register
(ECR)
DESIGNER
Henry Juskevicius
FIRM
NCR Corporation
MANUFACTURER
NCR Corporation
CLIENT
NCR Corporation

PRODUCT
Conceptual Classic Brass ECR
DESIGNERS
Bruce A. Quinn, Horng Jaan Lin,
Scott N. Barton, Mark Dawley
FIRM
NCR Corporation
MANUFACTURER
NCR Design Research
CLIENT
NCR Corporation

PRODUCT
Electric Bar Code Hand Labeler
EP-860
DESIGNER
Takeshi Matsumaru
FIRM
KAK Design Inc., Japan
MANUFACTURER
Shinsei Industries Co., Ltd.
CLIENT
Shinsei Industries Co., Ltd.

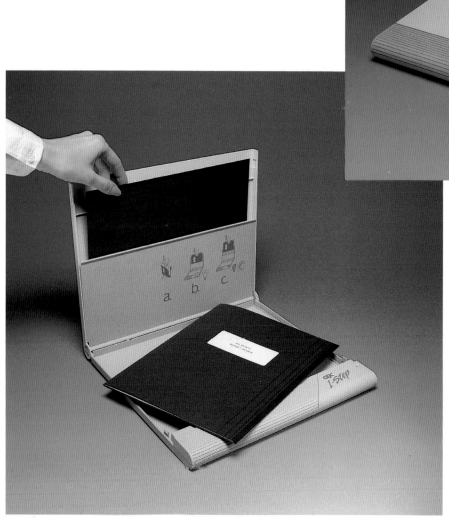

PRODUCT
1-Step
DESIGNER
Walter
FIRM
Herbst Lazar Bell Inc.
MANUFACTURER
General Binding Corporation
AWARD
ID Design Review
DESCRIPTION
One-step hot glue melt for binding

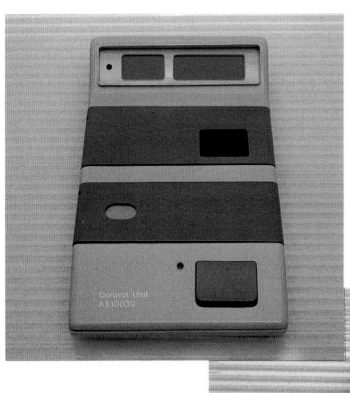

PRODUCT
Portable Electronic Voting Machine
DESIGNERS
Prof. A.G. Rao, Asst. Prof. Ravi
Poovaiah
MANUFACTURER
Bharat Electronics Ltd., India
CLIENT
Indian Election Commission

PRODUCT
Hand Scanner
DESIGNER
Daniele De Luliis
FIRM
ID TWO
CLIENT
Biometrics
DESCRIPTION
Verifies credit card holder identity
through hand characteristics.

CHAPTER 6

Perry King
Santiago Miranda
King-Miranda Associati

We are very concerned with the content of our designs because we are convinced that every object expresses signals to us—cultural, functional, market or status signals which stimulate responses, both on the functional and emotional levels.

This means that design isn't simply reconciling functional necessities and formal requirements into a harmonious whole, but is instead a process which tries to include communication between man and his artifacts. We call this "interactive design," the development of linguistic models which permit a real or potential relationship with the objects around us.

Our job as designers is to produce images which are consumed either collectively or singularly so that we can recognize ourselves in a product or environment. This is something men and women have always done. Just think of the savage who paints his hut. He is making a monument to the thoughts of his tribe or entire civilization. Just as today's western man, working on a different scale with newer methods, designs a monument to our civilization when he builds a high-rise bank in Hong Kong.

All artists have ambitions on an eternal level, absolute values which will last throughout time. We as designers however, are making very ephemeral creations destined to perish when economic development or technological progress overtakes them; nevertheless, they are tiny expressions of our civilization and we try to give them value. They must not be vulgar, meaningless, mean or useless.

•

Of course, function is a basic requirement of any design—an essential quality—but that does not mean that form must still follow function, if it ever did. Today for example, the freedom designers have in giving form to electronic equipment, where the components can be put into any reasonable shape, can be contrasted with the rigid restrictions of mechanical equipment where the positioning of levers and wheels is almost impossible to change.

I don't agree with the idea that the content of a design is limited by its physical functioning. Function is an incredibly complex service which embraces all our feelings. Nor must technology dictate to designers. It is a neutral force to be used as we wish, a large and malleable tool which the designer must use in order to achieve his or her aims.

I recently read of an experiment to precisely measure the distance from the earth to the moon. The experiment itself I find curious, but the technology that was used is wonderfully poetic. The idea was to send a beam of light from the earth to the moon and wait for its reflection to reach us; to receive moonlight not reflected from the sun but from our own light source—to have created moonlight—is a beautiful and dramatic thing!

•

People are becoming increasingly intolerant of uniform levels of lighting. They want to be able to establish their personal control over their environments, to create a sense of territory which is so important to well-being, not only in the office, but everywhere.

This means that in the future, lighting must be more flexible. In office spaces, those rows of fluorescent ceiling fittings that give a blank and even level of illumination will give way to fittings and systems which permit multiple light sources— fluorescent, halogen and incandescent—in an integrated whole. This creates a richness of color, perception and an absence of cold light. Flexible lighting which is easy to modify will become necessary in order to accommodate the rapid changes in office layouts which occur today.

Architects and designers are also catching on to the fact that it's very easy for them to control lighting. They don't have to settle for the standard ceiling light. Another important thing to understand is that shadow is not the opposite of light. It is a part of light—it is darkness, the absence of light. Shadow is very important, and architects have always used it in their compositions. So we should be providing the sort of lighting which enables architects to create depth and perspective.

•

I think you can tell a good design if you can immediately recognize that it has a certain inevitability about it. If it is something new that you feel had to come, then it stands a good chance of being a product that might last. If, on the other hand, you feel you have already seen it, then you probably have a more ordinary product that won't be as successful.

How do you design quality? By ensuring that, as much as possible, you are giving value for money. And by being convinced that consumers are much more sophisticated, open and aware of what is going on in the world than the marketing experts give them credit for. You know, people are exposed to exactly the same kind of visual pressures, the same kind of stimulation that we designers are exposed to. They are being influenced by the same cultural and financial pressures that affect us. They are at the forefront of all those movements —indeed they are those movements—which sociologists name and identify. Designers can help by making products and concepts which consumers will recognize as expressions of their needs.

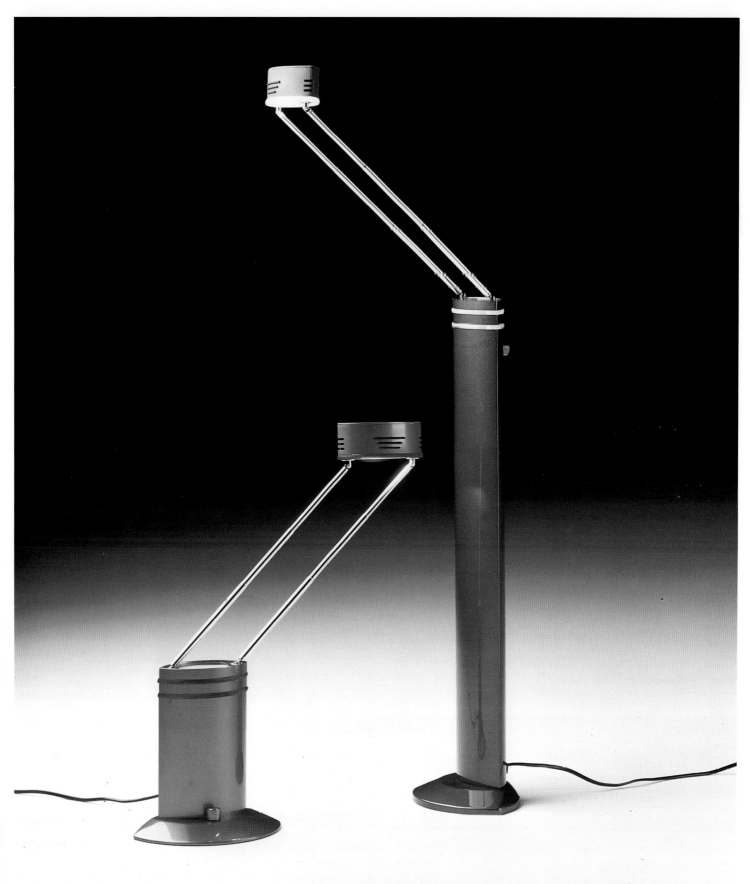

PRODUCT
Gina Desk & Floor Reading Lamp
DESIGNER
Antoni Flores
MANUFACTURER
Gargot–Disseny Mediterrani S.A.
MANUFACTURER
Gargot-Disseny Mediterrani S.A.,
Spain
CLIENT
Gargot–Disseny Mediterrani S.A.

PRODUCT
''Bolonia'' Table Lamp
DESIGNER
Josep Llusca
FIRM
Metalarte, Spain
MANUFACTURER
Roman Riera

PRODUCT
SL Kubo
DESIGNER
Philips Corporate Industrial Design

PRODUCT
Envelope Lamp
DESIGNER
David Tisdale
FIRM
David Tisdale Design Inc.
MANUFACTURER
David Tisdale Design Inc.

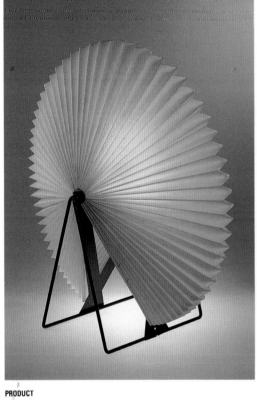

PRODUCT
Maya Fan Lamp
DESIGNER
Daniel T. Ebihara
CLIENT
Gallery 91
AWARD
1987 Design Review Selection

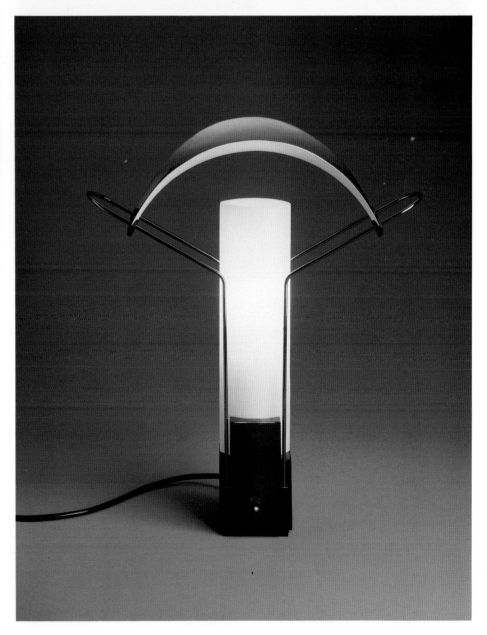

PRODUCT
''Palio'' Table Lamp
DESIGNERS
Perry King, Santiago Miranda
FIRM
King-Miranda Associati
MANUFACTURER
Arteluce
CLIENT
Arteluce
AWARD
1988 ID Review Selection

PRODUCT
Bugja Lamp
DESIGNER
Marco Aldegani
FIRM
Lamperti

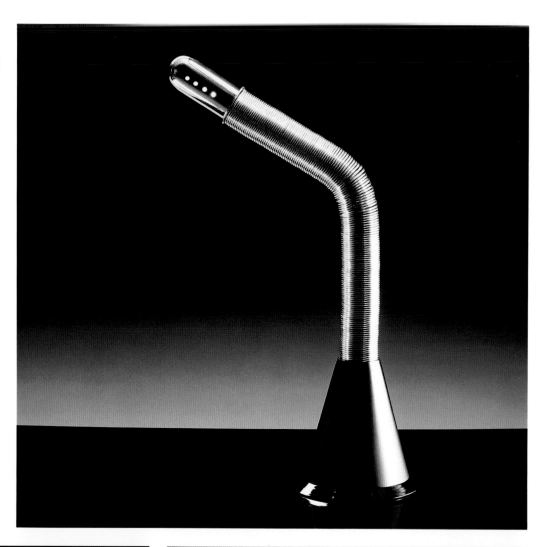

PRODUCT
''Saeta'' Lamp
DESIGNER
Josep Llusca
FIRM
Baluet, S.A., Spain
MANUFACTURER
Jordi Llusca

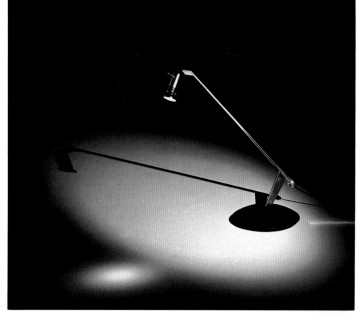

PRODUCT
Sigla T. Halogen Lamp
DESIGNER
Rene Kemna
FIRM
Sirrah, Imola (Italy); Innovative
Products for Interiors (U.S.A.)
CLIENT
See, Ltd.
AWARD
1987 ID Design Review Selection

PRODUCT
Tolomeo Halogen
DESIGNERS
Michele De Lucchi, Giancarlo
Fassina
FIRM
Artemide, Inc.
MANUFACTURER
Artemide, Inc.
AWARD
1987 SNAI Oscar Des Architectes
D'interieur

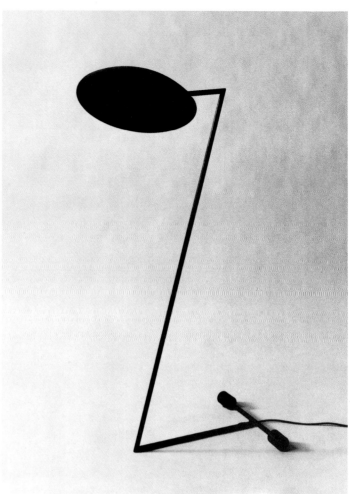

PRODUCT
''Zandt II''
DESIGNER
Kevin Gray

PRODUCT
Micro Halogen Lamp
DESIGNER
Pepsant-Ramon Begas
FIRM
Associate Designers, S.A., Spain
MANUFACTURER
Zelco Industries, Inc.
CLIENT
Zelco Industries, Inc.
AWARD
1987 ID Design Review Honorable
Mention

PRODUCT
Cheerioh
DESIGNERS
Susanne and Bernhard Dessecker
FIRM
Design M Ingo Maurer GmbH
MANUFACTURER
Design M Ingo Maurer GmbH

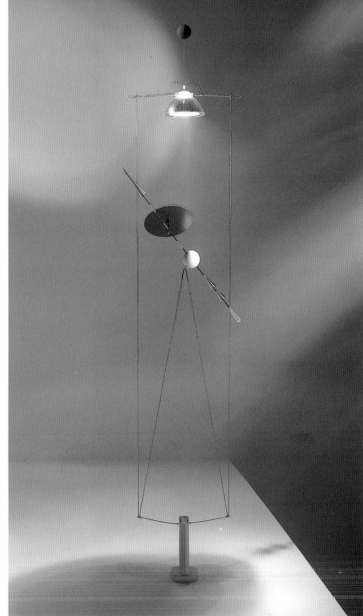

PRODUCT
Ilo-Ilu
DESIGNER
Ingo Maurer
FIRM
Design M Ingo Maurer GmbH
MANUFACTURER
Design M Ingo Maurer GmbH
AWARDS
1988 ID Design Review Selection;
1988 Design Contor Award,
Stuttgart, W. Germany

PRODUCT
Halogen Floor Lamp
FIRM
Matrix Product Design, Inc.
CLIENT.
Avatar, Canada
PHOTO
Miles Keller
AWARDS
1988 VIRTU Competition, Canada;
1988 ID Design Review Selection

PRODUCT
''Sail'' Floor Lamp
FIRM
Ken Keller Design

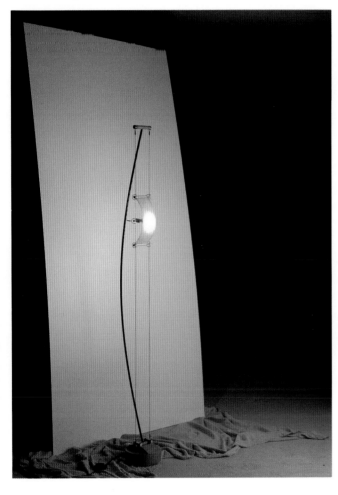

PRODUCT
Fukushu
DESIGNER
Ingo Maurer
FIRM
Design M Ingo Maurer GmbH
MANUFACTURER
Design M Ingo Maurer GmbH

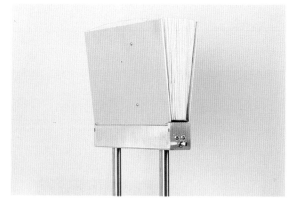

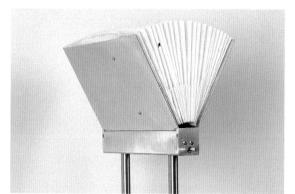

PRODUCT
Quahog Lamp
DESIGNERS
Leo J. Blackman, Lance D. Chantry
AWARDS
Arango Design Foundation Award;
1987 ID Design Review Selection

PRODUCT
Fantomas Wall-Floor Lamp
DESIGNER
David Baird
FIRM
Ziggurat
MANUFACTURER
Ziggurat
CLIENT
Ziggurat
PHOTO
Alan Linn

PRODUCT
Floor Lamp
DESIGNER
Shigeru Uchida
FIRM
Studio 80, Japan
MANUFACTURER
Chairs
CLIENT
Chairs and Gallery 91
AWARDS
Arango International Design
Competition; 1987 ID Design
Selection

PRODUCT
''Lotto Lamp''
DESIGNER
Forrest Myers
FIRM
Art et Industrie
MANUFACTURER
Art et Industrie/Forrest Myers

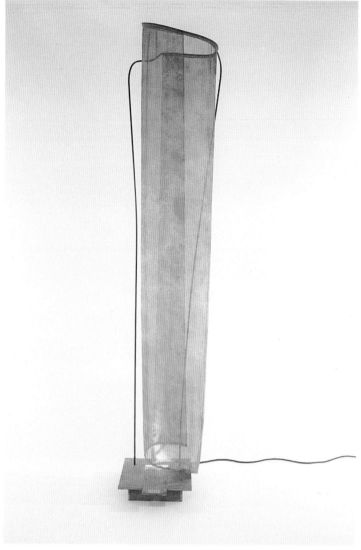

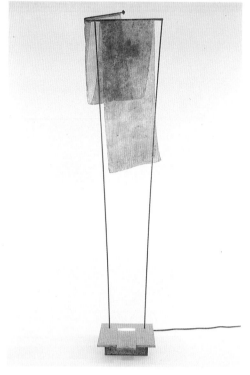

PRODUCT
''Mark, Lighten Up''
DESIGNER
Mark Parrish
FIRM
Art et Industrie
MANUFACTURER
Art et Industrie/Mark Parrish

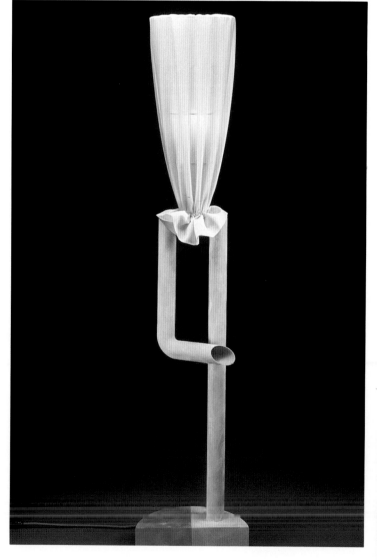

PRODUCT
Floor Lamp #11
DESIGNER
Jacqueline Ott

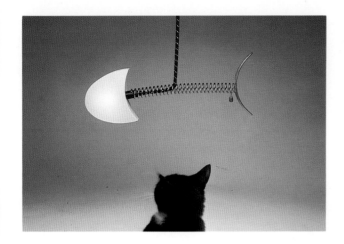

PRODUCT
Sardine Hanging Lamp
DESIGNERS
Tucker Viemeister, Lisa Krohn
FIRM
Smart Design
CLIENT
Gallery 91

PRODUCT
Lola
DESIGNERS
Paolo Rizzatto, Alberto Meda
MANUFACTURER
Luceplan

PRODUCT
Eagle Nest Floor Nest
DESIGNER
Jerry Kott
MANUFACTURER
Jerry Kott

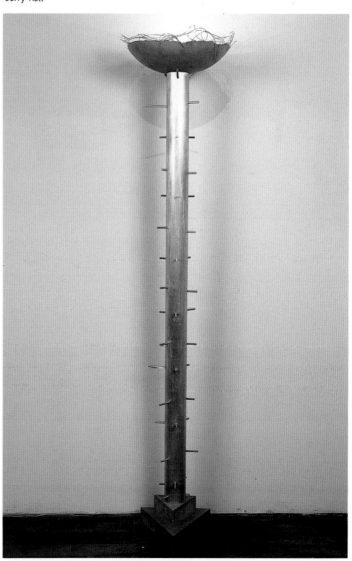

PRODUCT
D9 Wall
DESIGNERS
Paolo Rizzatto, Sandro Colbertaldo

PRODUCT
''Battery'' Wall Lamp
DESIGNER
Leo Blackman

PRODUCT
''Ares'' Floor and Wall Lamp
DESIGNER
Roberto Marcatti
MANUFACTURER
Noto, Italy

PRODUCT
Wall Fitting
DESIGNER
Sinya Okayama
FIRM:
Sinya Okayama Studio, Japan
MANUFACTURER
Sinya

PRODUCT
Expanded Line Network
DESIGNERS
Perry A. King, Santiago Miranda
FIRM
King-Miranda Associati
MANUFACTURER
Floss Incorporated

PRODUCT
KT845 Trapeze
DESIGNERS
Dan Dix, Tim Scherf
FIRM
Capri Lighting
MANUFACTURER
Capri Lighting
CLIENT
Capri Lighting

PRODUCT
Halogen Lighting Program
FIRM
ninaber/peters/krouwel
MANUFACTURER
Raak, The Netherlands

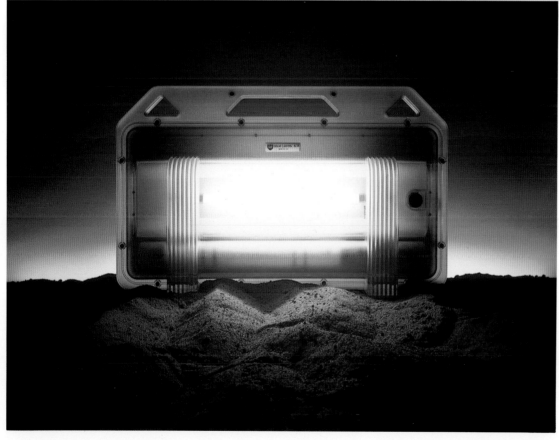

PRODUCT
Solar Lantern
DESIGNER
Hedda Beese
FIRM
Moggridge Associates, UK
CLIENT
British Petroleum
AWARDS
1988 ID Design Review Selection,
D&AD British Product Design Award

PRODUCT
''Valeria'' Ceiling Lamp
DESIGNER
Josep Llusca
FIRM
Metalarte, S.A., Spain
MANUFACTURER
Roman Riera

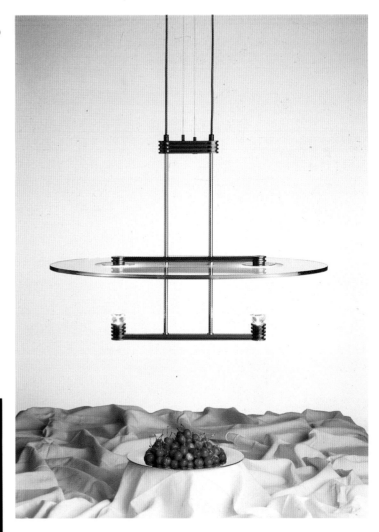

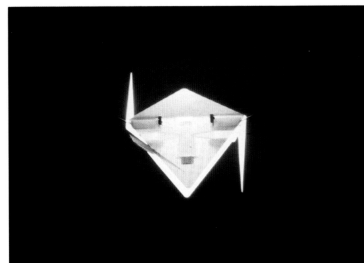

PRODUCT
Milvus Lamp
DESIGNER
Eric P. Chan
FIRM
Chan+Dolan Design Inc.
CLIENT
Chan+Dolan Design Inc.
AWARD
1987 Arango International Design
Exhibition

PRODUCT
''Arca''
DESIGNER
Xavier Solé
FIRM
Xavier Solé
CLIENT
Metalarte, S.A., Spain

PRODUCT
"Tilt 36"
DESIGNER
Doyle Crosby
FIRM
Boyd Lighting Company
PHOTO
Stone & Steccati

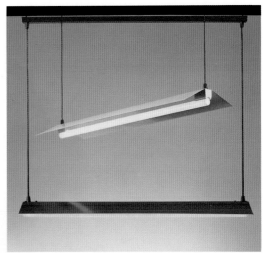

PRODUCT
Lineal
DESIGNER
Taller Uno

PRODUCT
Hanging Chandelier
DESIGNERS:
Ross Anderson, Walter Vogelsburg
FIRM
Anderson/Schwartz
MANUFACTURER
Solebury Forge
CLIENT
Ross Anderson

PRODUCT
Cobalt, Cobbler, Tear Pendants
DESIGNER
Piotr Sierakowski
FIRM
Koch + Lowy Inc.
MANUFACTURER
Koch + Lowy Inc.

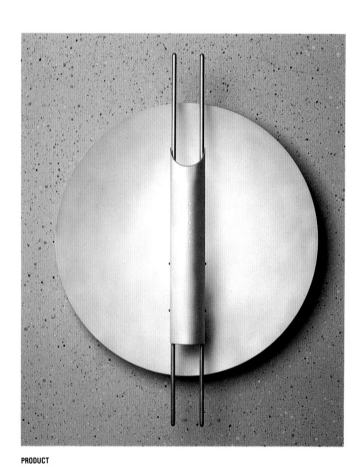

PRODUCT
Copernicus
DESIGNER
Piotr Sierakowski
FIRM
Koch + Lowy Inc.
CLIENT
Koch + Lowy Inc.
AWARD
1987 ID Design Review Selection

PRODUCT
''Sconce #2''
DESIGNER:
Thomas Hucker
FIRM
Thomas Hucker
MANUFACTURER
Thomas Hucker

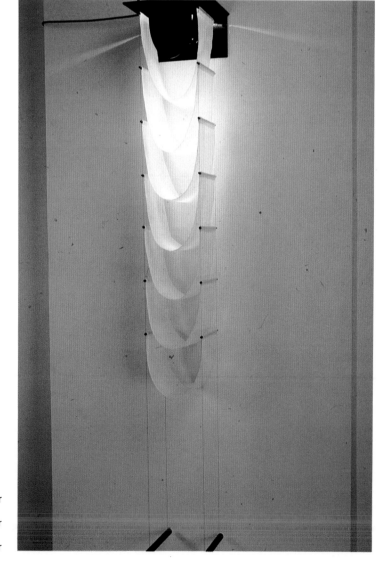

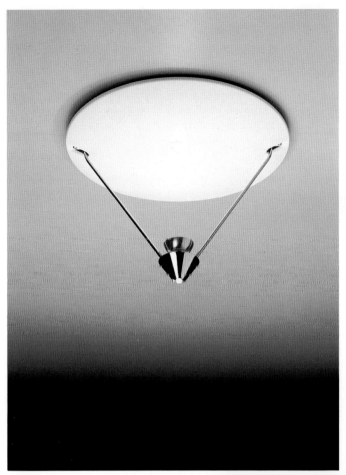

PRODUCT
Hanging Cone Lamp
DESIGNER
David Tisdale
FIRM
David Tisdale Design Inc.
MANUFACTURER
David Tisdale Design Inc.

PRODUCT
''Joia'' Ceiling Panel
DESIGNER
Josep Llusca
FIRM:
Metalarte, S.A., Spain
MANUFACTURER
Roman Riera

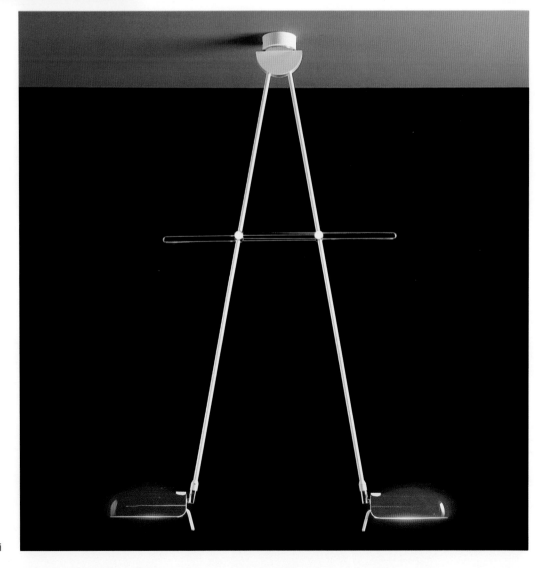

PRODUCT
Compasso 52/65
DESIGNERS
Luciano Balestrini, Paola Longhi

Massimo and **Lella Vignelli**
President and *Vice President*
Vignelli Associates

Lella Vignelli: When we design, we look for the minimal, the essential to make the object. We always search for pure geometry, not funny shapes. In the new design, there is a search for the strange and unfamiliar, which contradicts our philosophy.
Massimo Vignelli: We hate obsolescence as a concept, as a moral issue. And the way to avoid obsolescence is by designing things that work against being obsolete. And redefining the classics isn't the only way. It depends on the problem.

We started doing desk accessories when a manufacturer asked us to design a line. First we looked at the market and discovered there was a lot of heavy stuff, nothing really good or pure around. So we wanted to propose some simple yet accurate alternatives. Like our paper trays (page177). They are so simple, yet I could never find them. I used to make my own by folding and taping together cardboard, so I translated it into steel.

The desk pad has different channels for several functions. One for cigarettes or clips, one for pens or pencils. The diary fits into the module, and at the end of the day, you can take it out and put it into your pocket.

You see, I hate sloppiness and anything that contributes to visual clutter. I hate doors because they are always left open and they aren't meant to be. I like them closed. Likewise, if you provide the lid on a box, you can be sure it will always be left open because people are lazy. So I want a lid that closes the minute you're done with it. That's why I made desk containers with rubber lids. I don't care if they don't open all the way—they always close immediately. They have no springs because I hate mechanisms. You design what you are and my motto is: If you can't find it, design it.

•

LV: We are trying to say that design is different than fashion. Fashion becomes obsolete very quickly. Today, it's the same with some design because many manufacturers want more merchandise on the shelves, more movement of the market.
MV: Style is so transitory. And design is permanent. Or to put it another way, style changes and elegance is permanent. Ephemeral things are hardly ever elegant. They can be witty or fun, but not elegant.

Have you ever noticed that things that start with "post" are always transitory; have you ever heard of neo-elegance or post-elegance? No, because the neo's and the post's are appearances and appearances change. The essence is timeless. In the past, we were fanatics about these ideas. We lived in a more cohesive culture linked to more cohesive ideals. I think the '80s have cleared the way for the co-existence of ideas.

I say that obsolescence is disturbing as a moral issue more than from any other point of view because there's no need to design something that has been exhausted and adds nothing to function. Why design a new car every year? It takes so much effort. They say it keeps the economy together. Baloney! That's like saying it's necessary to make arms because they keep the economy alive. Baloney! You can keep the economy alive by designing things that are useful to society.

•

MV: I can answer any design question based on pens alone. The Flair marker, for example, is just what we are not.
This pen has been on the market for 15 or 20 years and I think it's terrible. It is nothing but a linear sequence of obsolescence. It's pure styling. On the Flair, you might think the ridges hold the cap, but no. When the cap comes off, you suddenly have four segments to the pen. For no reason. It's just sick engineering.
The beauty of the Pilot is that there's hardly anything about it you can't *not* like. Its form is a pure cylinder.
At the other extreme, you have an object like the Bulgari

—a silver case designed by someone who liked the function of the Flair but couldn't stand the look of it. You take the normal Flair—95 cents worth of ugliness—you put it into $300 worth of beauty, and you've got a memorable object, while the Flair, which you've used for 20 years, is completely forgettable. You can't even draw it because the mind rejects it!

Look at the Marco Zanuso pen. You'll find this pen 100 years from now because it has no age. It's sheer taste, elegance, civilization all put together. It has none of these emotional, transitory loads which have been so dear in the last few years—post-modernism, you know.

But notice, there is no loss of dignity between the Pilot and the Zanuso even though one costs $100 and the other 95 cents. And that is all design is about: to bring dignity into the hands of the people. As opposed to the Flair, which is insulting with its low-bred design. To me, bringing a sense of quality is what the social mission of design is all about. It's not flashiness. Post-modernism is on that flashy level.
LV: I don't agree. Memphis is interested in breaking out of the existing situation.
MV: But it falls into the same trap of obsolescence.
LV: It's forging another philosophy. It's breaking the mold in order to step forward. The problem is that the followers, not the leaders, don't know what the mold is. They are just following the form. They don't understand the philosophy or the ethics of design.
MV: Yes, but you know that form follows function; only idiots follow form.

PRODUCT
Sub Clock – ATC52 By Artimer
FIRM
Canetti Inc.
MANUFACTURER
Collector's Collection
CLIENT
Canetti Inc.

PRODUCT
Dual Face Travel Clock
DESIGNER
Takenobu Igarashi
FIRM
Igarashi Studio
MANUFACTURER
Tochigi Tokei Co., Ltd.
CLIENT
OUN Corporation

PRODUCT
Ball Clock
DESIGNER
Takenobu Igarashi
FIRM
Igarashi Studio
MANUFACTURER
Tochigi Tokei Co., Ltd.
CLIENT
OUN Corporation

PRODUCT
Pad and Pencil Depot
DESIGNER
Torben Holmback
FIRM
Holmback Design

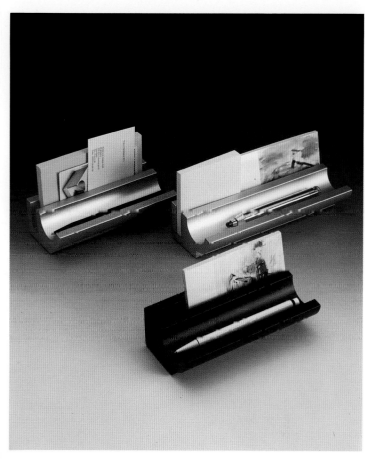

PRODUCT
Traveling Alarm Clocks
DESIGNER
Laura Handler
FIRM
Handler
MANUFACTURER
Pomellato, Italy
CLIENT
Pomellato

PRODUCT
Massimo Envelope Holder
DESIGNER
Alan Fletcher
FIRM
Pentagram
MANUFACTURER
OUN Corporation
CLIENT
OUN Corporation

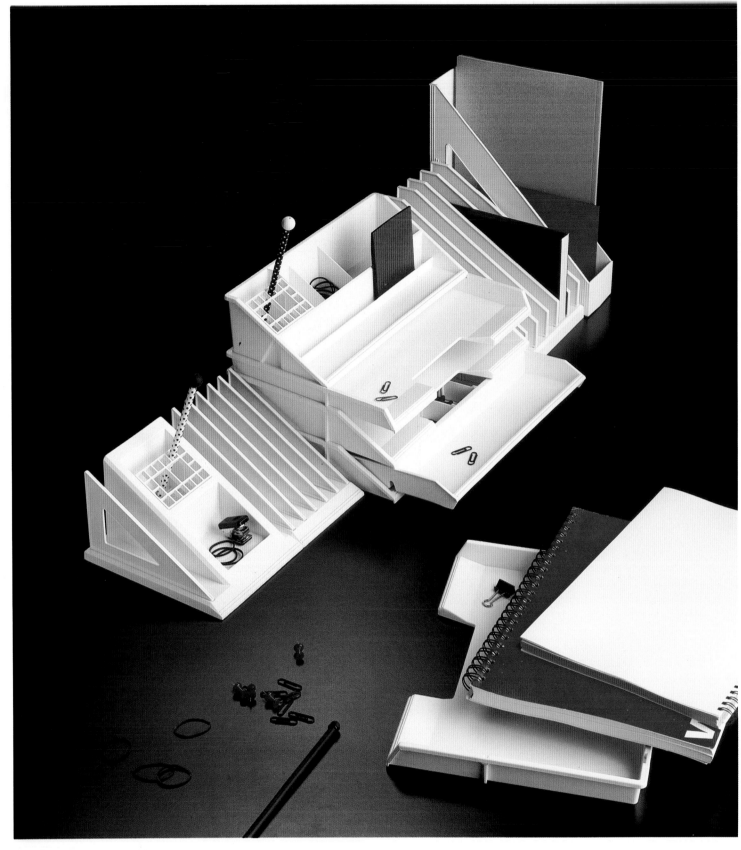

PRODUCT
Design-a-Space Home Office
Organizers
DESIGNERS
Bob Mervar, Pet Koloski, Tracy
Teague, Gerry Skulley, James
Couch, Tom David
FIRM
RichardsonSmith, Inc.
MANUFACTURER
Rubbermaid Inc.
CLIENT
Rubbermaid Inc.

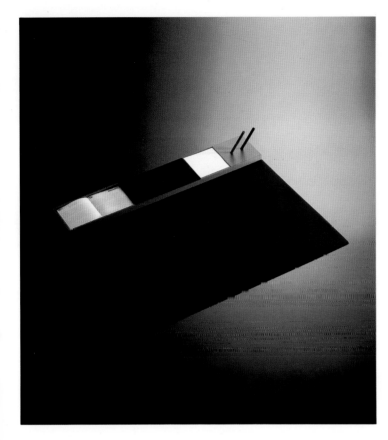

PRODUCT
Desk Oranizers With Desk Pad
DESIGNER
Maooimo Vignolli
FIRM
Vignelli Associates
MANUFACTURER
Hoyo Industry Co., Ltd.
CLIENT
OUN Corporation

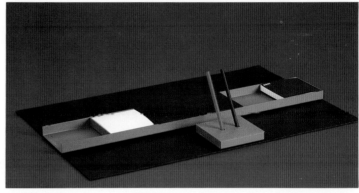

PRODUCT
Letter Tray
DESIGNER
Massimo Vignelli
FIRM
Vignelli Associates
MANUFACTURER
Hoyo Industry Co., Ltd.
CLIENT
OUN Corporation

PRODUCT
Curve Letter Holder
DESIGNER
David Wiener
FIRM
David Wiener Design

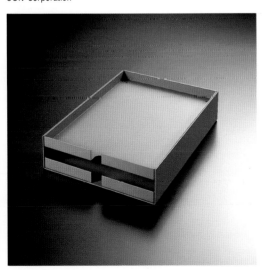

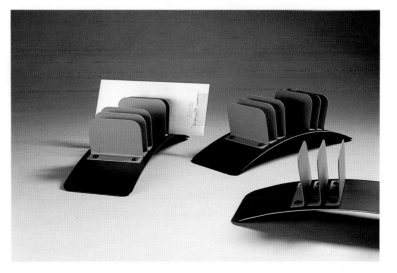

PRODUCT
GIII Canvas Basket
DESIGNER
Paul Rowan
FIRM
Umbra U.S.A. Inc.
MANUFACTURER
Umbra U.S.A. Inc.

PRODUCT
Cartons For Stationery
DESIGNER
Andree Putman
FIRM
Studio Ecart
MANUFACTURER
Cartoform

PRODUCT
Pencil Holder, Letter Holder,
In/Out Box
DESIGNER
Oscar Maschera, Claudia Serafini
FIRM
Marcovici Designs
MANUFACTURER
Arte Cudio

PRODUCT
Telescoping Graphics Tube
DESIGNER
Bruno Morassutti
MANUFACTURER
Arte Cuoio
CLIENT
Marcovici Designs

PRODUCT
Desk Accessories
DESIGNERS
Lloyd Schwan, Lyn Godley
FIRM
Godley-Schwan
MANUFACTURER
Godley-Schwan

PRODUCT
Resentel Attache Case
DESIGNER
Michel Dallaire
FIRM
Michel Dallaire Designers Inc.
MANUFACTURER
La Compagnie Resentel Ltee
AWARD
Canada Award For Excellence

PRODUCT
Year'Round Calendar
DESIGNER
Patrick Florville
FIRM
Florville Design & Analysis, Inc.
MANUFACTURER
Bennett Plastics
CLIENT
Florville Design & Analysis, Inc.
AWARDS:
1988 Package Design Council; 1988
AIGA; 1987 D.E.S.I.

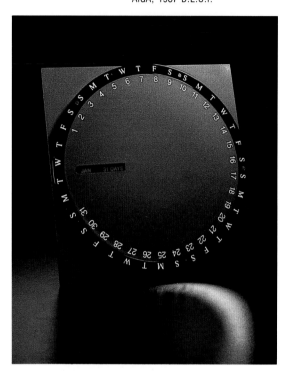

PRODUCT
''Sof-Stone'' Desk Accessory
Collection
DESIGNER
Tom Janicz
FIRM
Tom Janicz Design Group
MANUFACTURER
Knoll International
AWARD
1987 ROSCOE Award

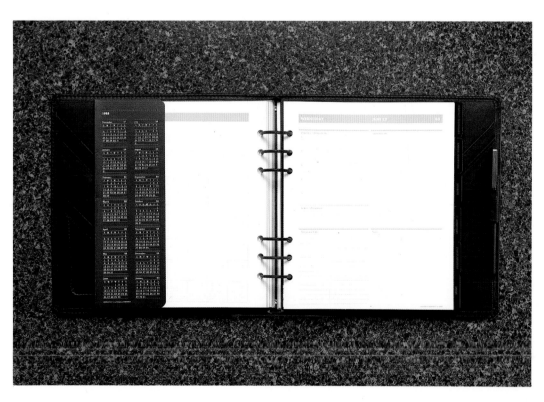

PRODUCT
Novadatum Personal Time Planner
DESIGNERS
Marilyn Hite, Gilberto Schaefer
FIRM
Novadatum
MANUFACTURER
Novatrix
CLIENT
Marcovici Designs

PRODUCT
Tape Flag Dispenser
DESIGNERS
Alden R. Miles, Bruce E. Nelson,
James C. Nygard
FIRM
3M Hardgoods Technology Center/
Industrial Design
MANUFACTURER
3M Commercial Office Supply
Division
CLIENT
3M Commercial Office Supply
Division
AWARD:
1988 ID Design Review Selection

PRODUCT
Planner
DESIGNER
James L. Fournier
FIRM
JLF Designs
MANUFACTURER
Bennington Leather Inc.
AWARD
Accent On Design Award

PRODUCT
''Profile'' Calendar Platform
DESIGNER
Torben Holmback
FIRM
Holmback Design, Denmark

PRODUCT
''Trank'' Floppy Disk Case
DESIGNERS
Michio Takechi, Masafumi Miyamoto
FIRM
Hirano & Associates, Inc.
MANUFACTURER
King Jim Co., Ltd.
CLIENT
King Jim Co., Ltd.
AWARD
Good Design Prize (Japan)

PRODUCT
''Space 330 and Space 540''
Floppy Disk Containers
DESIGNERS
Isao Hosoe, Alessio Pozzoli
FIRM
Isao Hosoe Design
MANUFACTURER
Massplast
CLIENT
Massplast/MEE
AWARD
1987 SMAU Industrial Design Prize

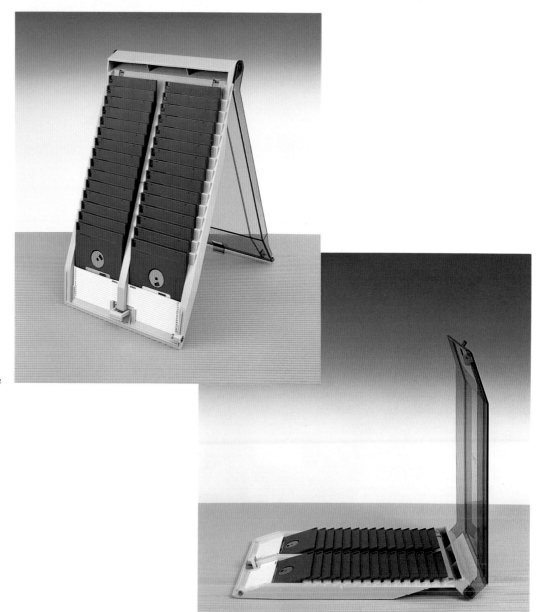

PRODUCT
Design Unique: Matte Black Ball
Point Pen
DESIGNER
Gerd A. Müller
FIRM
Lamy

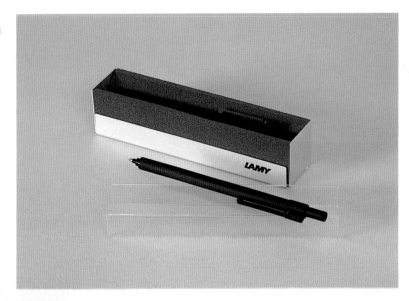

PRODUCT
Pen
DESIGNERS
Laura Handler, Lawrence Rosenberg
FIRM
Handler
MANUFACTURER
Pomellato, Italy
CLIENT
Pomellato

PRODUCT
"Expand" Floppy Disk File
DESIGNER
Michio Takechi
FIRM
Hirano & Associates, Inc.
MANUFACTURER
King Jim Co., Ltd.
CLIENT
King Jim Co., Ltd.
AWARD
1987 Good Design Prize (Japan)

PRODUCT
The Black Collection
DESIGNER
Nicolai Canetti
FIRM
Canetti Inc.
MANUFACTURER
Canetti Inc.
CLIENT
Canetti Inc.

PRODUCT
''Letapet 101'' Letter Opener
DESIGNERS
Katsuji Muraki, Norio Wada
FIRM
Hirano Shokai Co., Ltd.
MANUFACTURER
Meiko Shokai Co., Ltd.
CLIENT
Meiko Shokai Co., Ltd.
AWARDS
1987 Good Design Prize (Japan);
1988 ''IF'' Award, W. Germany

PRODUCT
Mark Maker Embosser
DESIGNERS
Robert W. Schram, Cameron L.
Fink, Anthony J. Gentile
FIRM:
Sterling Marking Products, Inc.,
Canada
MANUFACTURER:
Sterling Marking Products, Inc.
AWARD:
Plast-Ex '86, Canada Awards for
Excellence Silver Medal

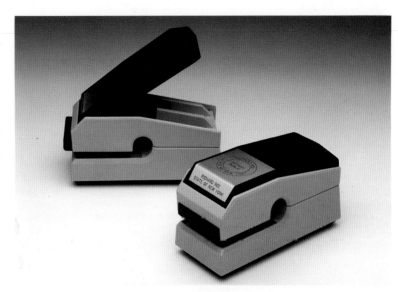

PRODUCT
Battery Pencil Sharpener/Holder
DESIGNER
Kenneth Grange
FIRM
Pentagram Design Limited
MANUFACTURER
Ishimitsu Kinzoku Kogyo Co., Ltd.
Toshiba Battery Co., Ltd.
CLIENT
OUN Corporation

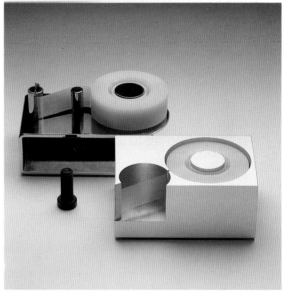

PRODUCT
Tape Tool & Tape Block
DESIGNER:
Torben Holmbäck
FIRM:
Holmback Design, Denmark
AWARD:
G – Prize For Good Design, Japan

PRODUCT:
''Stamp-Ever'' Self-Inking Stamper
FIRM:
Bartlett Design Assoc., Inc.
AWARD:
1988 ID Design Review Honorable
Mention

CHAPTER 8

Robert Blaich
Managing Director for Design
Philips

When talking about the best designs of domestic appliances and tools, one must understand that in the last years, this category has not been the hotbed of innovation compared to consumer electronics or computers. Often these products can only be distinguished by their visual aesthetics or by a few bells and whistles.

Still, there is no doubt in my mind that in the past decade design leadership in this category has come from Europe. Manufacturers such as Braun, Krups and Philips have made what the U.S. press calls "Euro-style" products of high-quality and high-design for some time. Only recently have we seen American manufacturers getting on the "Euro-style" bandwagon. The Japanese are now fast followers, and they have even introduced a few innovations, such as the small bread-making machine.

Overall, I think the European designs are superior because the Europeans have had a long culture of eating as opposed to the relatively new fast food culture of the USA. That long history has spawned many specialized products. For example, Philips is the world's largest producer of coffee machines and we design them to deal with the different ways people around the world prepare coffee. We make small machines for singles or couples, a "Cafe Therm" for eight to 10 cups which can be transported to the table or to work. Another product, the "Cafe Latte" combines coffee and warm milk for the French taste.

In home-care products however, there have been innovations from the U.S., in particular the Black and Decker "Dustbuster" hand-vacuum which has since been emulated around the world. American irons and personal care products are also of high quality, but tend to lack European design flair.

In tools, the U.S. has also led the category with efficient, well-designed products, but the new offerings from Japan are the most exciting. They are small, portable, beautifully crafted tool kits (some even come in pocket sizes), often in well-conceived carrying cases. Often they have sculptural forms, atypical colors and inventive packaging. If they continue to reinterpret traditional tools in new materials, I think the Japanese could take leadership in this category.

•

In the future I think we are going to see "electronification," the ability of appliances or tools to give us feedback. There is already a new electronic "tapeless measure" that measures space and distance with electronic impulses. Other small appliances can even be programmed to talk back to their users.

We will also be heading toward the age of the rechargeable appliance. While there are some currently on the market, you can expect this to be major growth area, in both single-and multi-purpose products. For example, a power unit that will be able to feed different appliances—a beater, a knife, a stirrer, or an opener—will be standard fare in the kitchen.

But this rapid product development poses a problem for the designer. The pace has increased to such an extent that the designer doesn't have much time to be thoughtful. Audio equipment that used to take three years to develop now takes nine months. And in many cases, designers never talk to end-users. Information is filtered through sales and management people who are responding to information they have gathered. It's common to hear, "This product sold well last year, so make another one just like it, which looks differently and costs 10% less." Product development has become like archeology, digging into the past for information instead of looking to the future. Designers must become more proactive than reactive. And successful solutions come from knowing what the end-user needs.

Another thing—it's one thing to design a product and another to sell it. I feel very strongly that design schools should require classes in public speaking so that students can learn to articulate verbally what they have articulated on paper in their designs. As my mentor, Charles Eames, used to say, "in the statement of the problem lies the solution."

•

As we move into international marketing, we can see that while many products are global, they are also very culturally specific. People in Japan, China, Malaysia, India and Italy all eat a lot of rice, but they prepare it quite differently; thus a rice cooker must be designed to accommodate these variations. The designer must study and understand the cultural climate he or she is designing for.

Who is the highest authority in design today, the designer, the manufacturer or the market? None of the above and all of the above. Today the field requires a team effort with designers, marketers, and engineers as equals. And this doesn't necessarily mean we must compromise. To paraphrase Eames, we can accept constraints but not compromises. If the project brief is well-stated, and the designer brings his or her full creative effort and skills to bear, then compromise is not necessary.

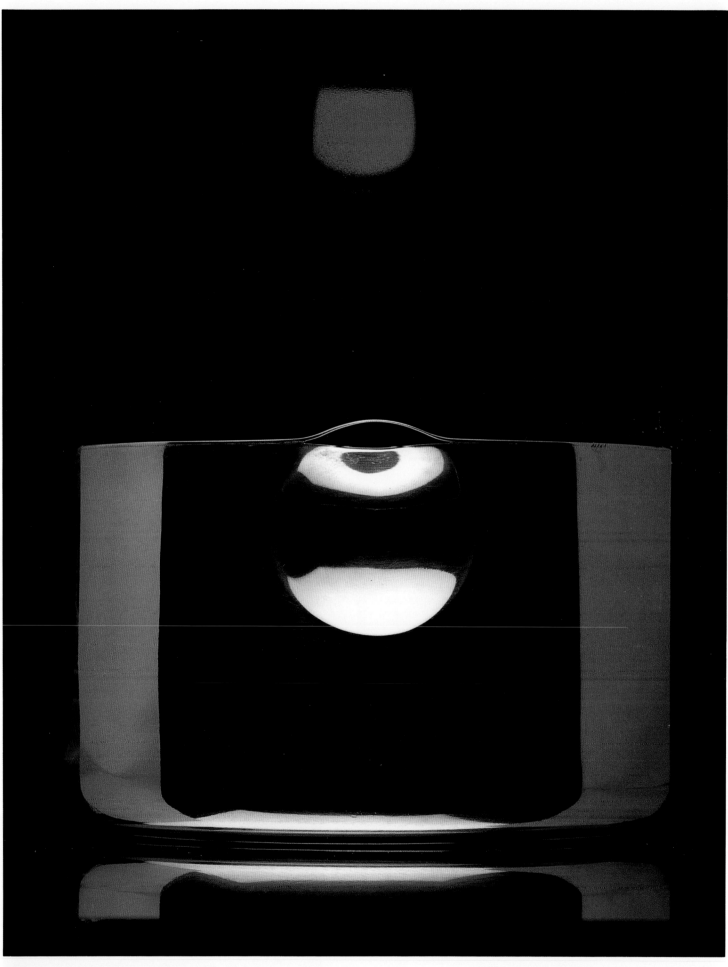

PRODUCT
Porcelli Tea Kettle
DESIGNER
V. Lorenzo Porcelli
MANUFACTURER
Dansk International

PRODUCT
Neoteric Tools
DESIGNER
Takagi Tools Inc., Japan
FIRM
Takagi Tools, Inc.
MANUFACTURER
Takagi Tools, Inc.

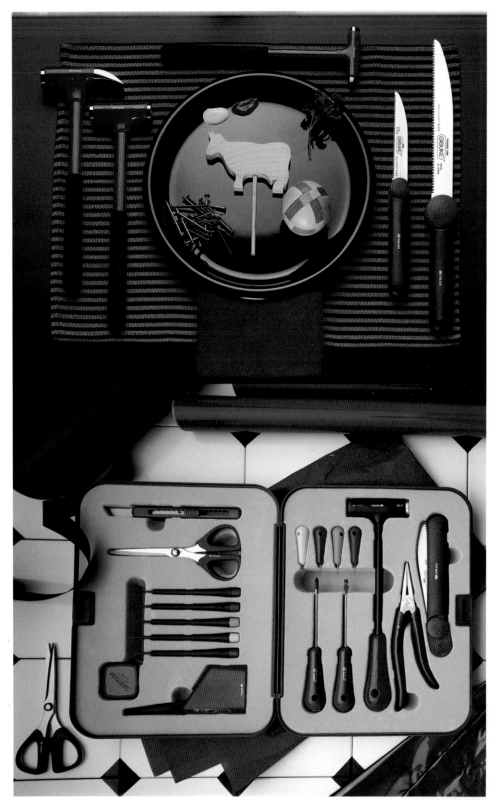

PRODUCT
Rawlings Combination Level/
Protractor
DESIGNERS
Peter W. Bressler, John D.
Coleman, P. Ken Rossi, Steven
Guerra
FIRM
Bresslergroup
MANUFACTURER
G. Rawlings, Inc.
CLIENT
G. Rawlings, Inc.
AWARD
1988 Annual ID Design Review
Honorable Mention

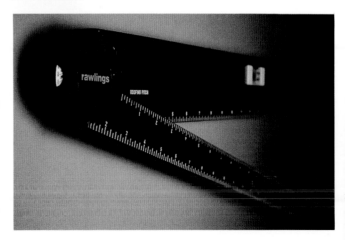

PRODUCT
Xcelite Tool Cases–Models MPX,
SMX, SMWX
DESIGNER
David Chapin
FIRM
CooperTools
MANUFACTURER
CooperTools–Xcelite Division
CLIENT
CooperTools
PHOTO
Duane Salstrand

PRODUCT
Turner Refillable Propane Torch
DESIGNERS
David Chapin, Gil Farnham
FIRM
CooperTools
MANUFACTURER
CooperTools – Turner Division
CLIENT
CooperTools
PHOTO
Duane Salstrand

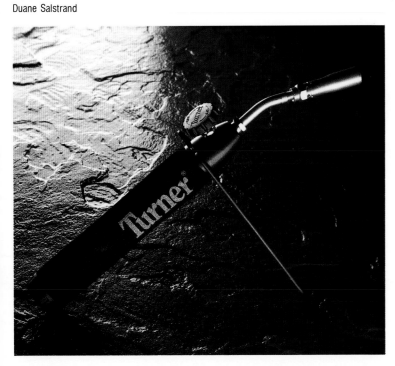

PRODUCT
Weller 8200 Soldering Gun–
Prototype
DESIGNER
David Chapin
FIRM
CooperTools
MANUFACTURER
CooperTools–Weller Division
CLIENT
CooperTools
PHOTO
Duane Salstrand

PRODUCT
Haws Copper Cans
FIRM
Smith & Hawken

PRODUCT
Gardena Multi Pattern Gun
FIRM
Smith & Hawken

PRODUCT
Power Roller Plus
DESIGNERS
David Miller, Thomas Pendleton,
Robert Dawson
FIRM
King–Casey, Inc.
MANUFACTURER
Wagner
CLIENT
Wagner

PRODUCT
IBM 7575 Manipulator
DESIGNER
Randall W. Martin
FIRM
IBM
MANUFACTURER
IBM
CLIENT
IBM

PRODUCT
''Hang Fast'' Wall Anchoring
System
DESIGNERS
Michael Ballone, Edward Levy,
Edward Meisner
FIRM
Innovations & Development, Inc.
CLIENT
Parker Group, Sears Roebuck & Co.
DESCRIPTION:
Hangs objects without drilling.

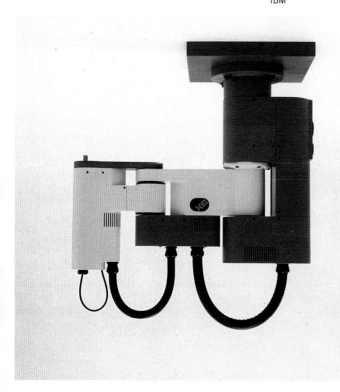

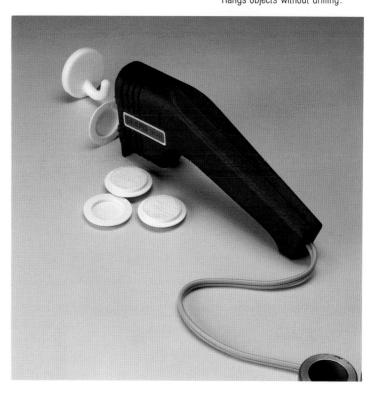

PRODUCT
Tile Cutter
DESIGNERS
Joan Sunyol, Josep Novell
FIRM
Via Design S.A.
MANUFACTURER
Germans Boado, S.A., Spain
CLIENT
Germans Boada, S.A.
AWARD
EUROPALIA 1986

PRODUCT
Wiss Ergonomic Shears
DESIGNER
David Chapin
FIRM
CooperTools
MANUFACTURER
CooperTools—Wiss Division
CLIENT
CooperTools
PHOTO
Duane Salstrand

PRODUCT
All Purpose Outdoor Knife
DESIGNER
Greg Hicks
FIRM
Uro Designs
MANUFACTURER
Donnie Beaver
CLIENT
Uro Designs

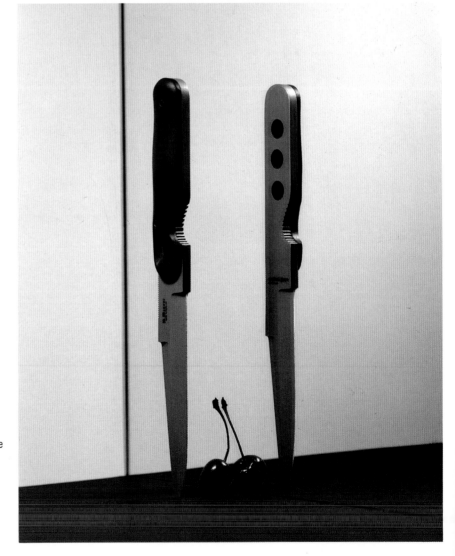

PRODUCT
Roll Cutter
DESIGNER
Sava Cvek
FIRM
Sava Cvek Associates
MANUFACTURER
Quadd Inc.
CLIENT
Quadd Inc.

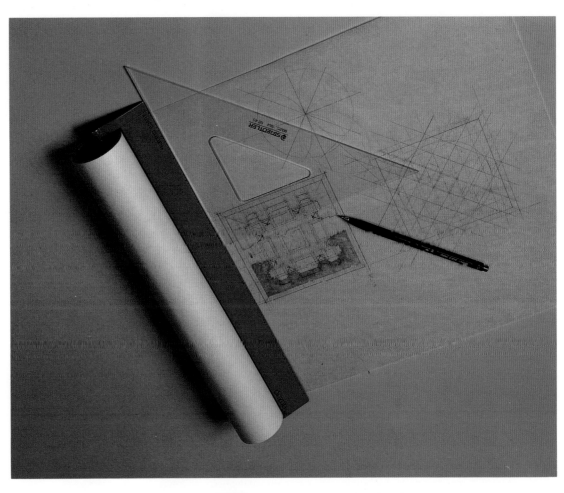

PRODUCT
Matchless Spinning Wheel
DESIGNERS
Barry and Daniel Schacht
FIRM
Schacht Spindle Co., Inc.

PRODUCT
Interlock Knives
FIRM
DCA Design International Limited
MANUFACTURER
Stanley Tools, UK
CLIENT
Stanley Tools

PRODUCT
''Toast–Modernism''
DESIGNER
Earl Gee
FIRM
Mark Anderson Design
MANUFACTURER
One Of A Kind
CLIENT
One Of A Kind

PRODUCT
Professional Toaster
DESIGNER
Dualit, Ltd.
FIRM
Dualit, Ltd.
MANUFACTURER
Dualit, Ltd.
CLIENT
Waring Products Division

PRODUCT
''Slice It''
DESIGNER
Herr Gunter Storsberg
FIRM
Robert Krups Stiftung & Co. KG
MANUFACTURER
Robert Krups, W. Germany

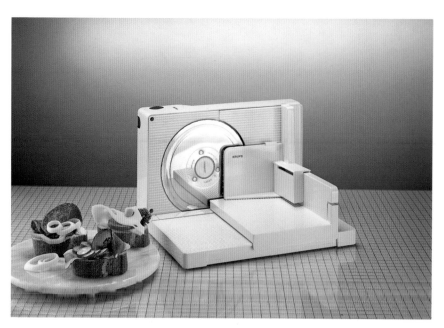

PRODUCT
Dallaire Design BBQ Tool Set
DESIGNER
Michel Dallaire
FIRM
Michel Dallaire Designers Inc.
MANUFACTURER
Dallaire Combey Inc., Canada
CLIENT
Dallaire Combey Inc.
AWARDS
1987 SAD Bronze, Paris; 1988 ID
Design Review Honorable Mention

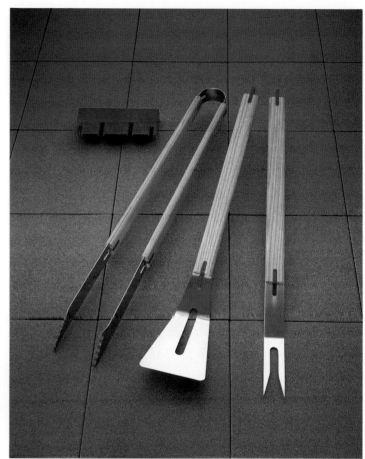

PRODUCT
Bottle Opener
DESIGNER
Emiel Vaasen
FIRM
Duo Design
MANUFACTURER
Duo Design
CLIENT
Kikkerland Co.

PRODUCT
Giotta Can Opener
DESIGNERS
Davide Mercatali, Paolo Pedrizzetti
FIRM
Davide Mercatali and Paolo
Pedrizzetti
MANUFACTURER
ICOM S.A.S., Italy
CLIENT
ICOM S.A.S.
AWARD
1987 Compasso D'oro

PRODUCT
Ice Cream Maker
FIRM
Philips Home Products

PRODUCT
Braun Juice Extractor MP80
DESIGNER
H. Kahlcke
FIRM
Braun, AG, W. Germany
MANUFACTURER
Braun AG
CLIENT
Braun, Inc.

PRODUCT
Electronic Kitchen Scale
DESIGNER
Philips Corporate Industrial Design
FIRM
Philips
MANUFACTURER
Philips
CLIENT
Philips
DESCRIPTION
Digital memory allows ingredients to
be measured separately without
removing previous item.

PRODUCT
Pasta Maker
DESIGNER
Richard Appleby
FIRM
Atlantic Design

PRODUCT
Mixer
FIRM
Philips Home Products
MANUFACTURER
Philips

PRODUCT
Carnival Drinks Maker
DESIGNERS
Barrie Weaver, Michael Taylor
FIRM
Roberts Weaver Design Limited, UK
MANUFACTURER
Sodastream Ltd.
CLIENT
Sodastream Ltd.
DESCRIPTION:
Home carbonation system.

PRODUCT
Spacemaker Plus
DESIGNER
Black & Decker Staff
FIRM
Black & Decker and Group Four
AWARD
1988 IDEA Award

PRODUCT
Microwave Oven
DESIGNER
Philips Corporate Industrial Design
FIRM
Philips

PRODUCT
Braun Multipractic Hand Blender
MR30
DESIGNER
L. Littmann
FIRM:
Hill, Holliday Public Relations
MANUFACTURER
Braun AG
CLIENT
Braun, Inc.

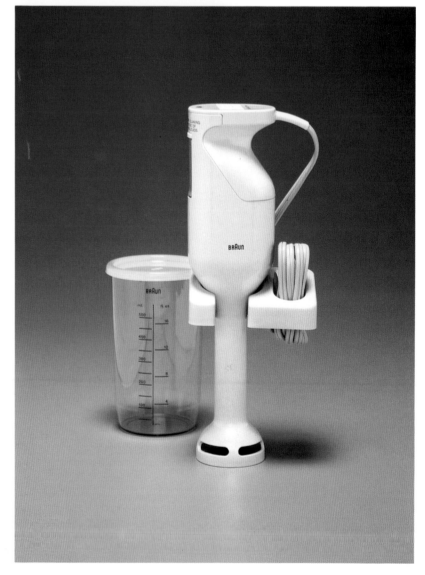

PRODUCT
''Cafe-Presso''
DESIGNER
Mr. Haslacher
FIRM
Robert Krups Stiftung & Co. KG
MANUFACTURER
Eugster, Switzerland

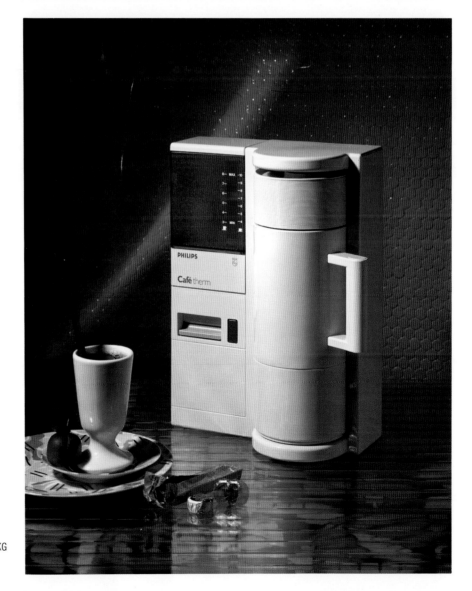

PRODUCT
''Espresso Mini'' Espresso/
Cappuccino Machine #963
DESIGNER
Herr Seiffert
FIRM
Robert Krups Stiftung & Co. KG
MANUFACTURER
Eugster, Switzerland

PRODUCT
K600 Horn Kettle
DESIGNER
Yoshiharu Fuwa
FIRM
Umbra U.S.A. Inc.
MANUFACTURER
Cookvessel, Japan
AWARD
Best Product, 1988 Frankfurt Fair

PRODUCT
Chantal Tea-Kettle
DESIGNER
Heida Thurlow
FIRM
Lentrade, Inc.
MANUFACTURER
Lentrade, Inc.

PRODUCT
''La Cupola'' Caffettiera
DESIGNER
Aldo Rossi
FIRM
Alessi, Italy
MANUFACTURER
Alessi

PRODUCT
T42 The Kettle That Whistles, ''Tea
For Two''
DESIGNER
Charles Hutter
FIRM
Physical Systems, Inc.
MANUFACTURER
Metrokane
CLIENT
Metrokane

PRODUCT
Braun Aromaster Coffeemaker With
Digital Clock Timer KF80BGF And
Gold Filter
DESIGNER
H. Kahlcke
FIRM
Braun, AG
MANUFACTURER
Braun, AG, W. Germany
CLIENT
Braun, Inc.

PRODUCT
Rowenta Espresso/Cappuccino
Machine ES-01B
DESIGNER
Franz Stutzer
FIRM
Rowenta
MANUFACTURER
Rowenta
CLIENT
Rowenta

PRODUCT
Sugar And Creamer Set
DESIGNER
Michael Graves
FIRM
Michael Graves, Architect
MANUFACTURER
Alessi
CLIENT
Alessi

PRODUCT
Serie ''Toda'' Bath Accessories
DESIGNER
Josep Llusca
FIRM
Uraldi, Spain
MANUFACTURER
Jose Antonio Echeverria

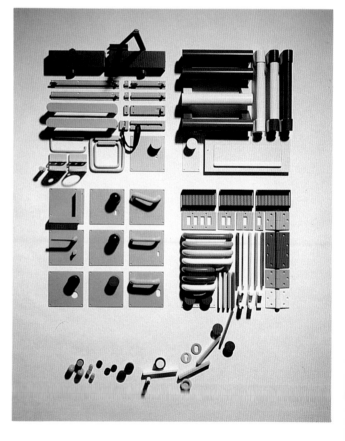

PRODUCT:
Modric ''Spectra'' Color System
DESIGNER:
Alan Tye R.D.I.
FIRM:
Alan Tye Design
MANUFACTURER:
G & S Allgood Ltd. (UK), Modric
Inc. (U.S.A.)
CLIENT:
G & S Allgood Ltd., Modric Inc.
AWARD:
1988 ROSCOE Award

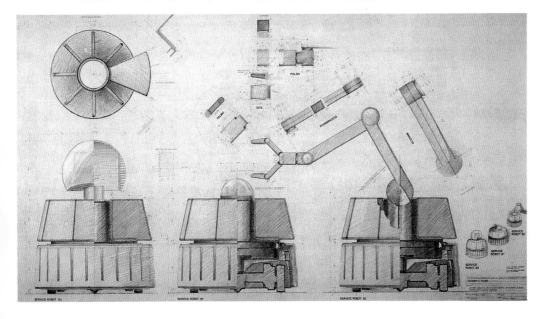

PRODUCT
Modulus Domestic Robot
DESIGNERS
Isao Hosoe, Donato Greco, Ann
Marinelli, Alessio Pozzoli
FIRM
Isao Hosoe Design
MANUFACTURER
Sirius S.p.A., Italy
CLIENT
Sirius

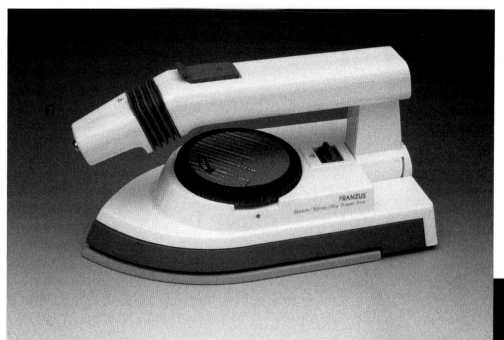

PRODUCT
Steam/Spray/Dry Travel Iron
DESIGNERS
William Guo, Hiroaki Kozu, Michael Young
FIRM
Michael W. Young Associates, Inc.
MANUFACTURER
Franzus Co. Inc.
CLIENT
Franzus Co. Inc.

PRODUCT
Compact Laundry
DESIGNER
Design Department Home Appliance Sector
FIRM
Matsushita Electric Industrial Co., Ltd., Japan
MANUFACTURER
Matsushita Electric Industrial Co., Ltd.

PRODUCT
Rowenta Steambrush Garment
Steamer With Crease Accessory
DESIGNER
Franz Stützer
FIRM
Rowenta
MANUFACTURER
Rowenta
CLIENT
Rowenta

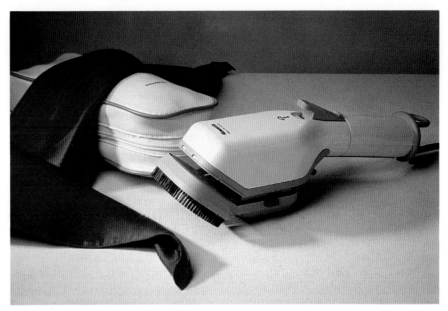

PRODUCT
HP4333 Hairdryer
DESIGNER
Philips Corporate Industrial Design
FIRM
Philips, The Netherlands

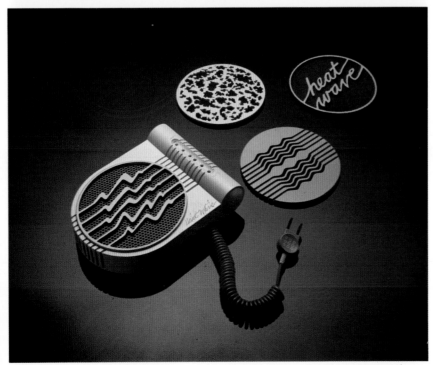

PRODUCT
Heatwave Hairdryer – Concept
DESIGNERS
Rainer Teufel, Gregg Davis, Paul
Kolada, Diana Woehnl
FIRM
Design Centrel
PHOTO
Larry Friar

PRODUCT
Waterbeads (Shower Curtain Hooks)
DESIGNERS
Laura Handler, Lawrence Rosenberg
FIRM
Handler
MANUFACTURER
Waterware, Inc.
CLIENT
Waterware, Inc.

PRODUCT
''Multirapid'' Pressure Cooker
DESIGNER
Josep Llusca
FIRM
Radar, S. Loop, Spain
MANUFACTURER
Pedro Lizarralde

PRODUCT
Odeon Taps
DESIGNERS
Davide Mercatali, Paolo Pedrizzetti
FIRM
Davide Mercatali and Paolo
Pedrizzetti
MANUFACTURER
F.LLI Fantini S.p.A.
CLIENT
F.LLI Fantini S.p.A.

PRODUCT
Chantal SL 8-piece Cookware Set
DESIGNER
Heida Thurlow
FIRM
Lentrade, Inc.
MANUFACTURER
Lentrade, Inc.

PRODUCT
Concept for Microwave Cookware
DESIGNERS
Sandra Dwyer, Chris Dykes, Lisa
Herring, Harry Strauss, Ed Wachter
FIRM
Philadelphia College of Art
CLIENT
Black & Decker, student
collaboration

PRODUCT
Food Keepers
DESIGNERS
Michael Ballone, Ronald Charriez,
Edward Meisner
FIRM
Innovations & Development, Inc.
MANUFACTURER
Anchor Hocking, Plastics Inc.
DESCRIPTION
Stores leftovers in refrigerator or
freezer which can then be reheated
in microwave or conventional oven.

PRODUCT
Vivitar Series 1 Binocular Line
DESIGNER
Steven Shull
FIRM
Hanimex–Vivitar Group
MANUFACTURER
Hoya Optical
CLIENT
Vivitar Corporation
AWARDS
1988 Stuttgart Design Center, 1988
Annual ID Design Review Selection

PRODUCT
Tekna-Lite 2AA With Battery Life
Indicator (BLI)
DESIGNER
Ralph Osterhout
FIRM
Tekna
MANUFACTURER
Tekna
DESCRIPTION
Shows life of battery via LED
indicator.

PRODUCT
Sigmalite Flashlight
DESIGNERS
Douglas Paige, Andrea Loosen
FIRM
Ron Loosen Associates
MANUFACTURER
LiteTek International
CLIENT
LiteTek International

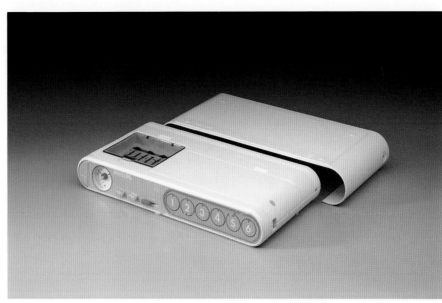

PRODUCT
Electric Fan-Forced Heater FE12LID
DESIGNER
Matsushita Seiko Co., Ltd.
Industrial Design Dept
FIRM
Matsushita Seiko Co., Ltd.

PRODUCT
Electronic Clock Radio/Space Saver-
D3996
DESIGNER
Philips Corporate Industrial Design
FIRM
Philips

PRODUCT
Thin-Air Fan
DESIGNERS
Ralph Osterhout, Steve Siefert
FIRM
Tekna
MANUFACTURER
Tekna
AWARD
Accent's New Product Award, 1988
Annual ID Design Review Selection

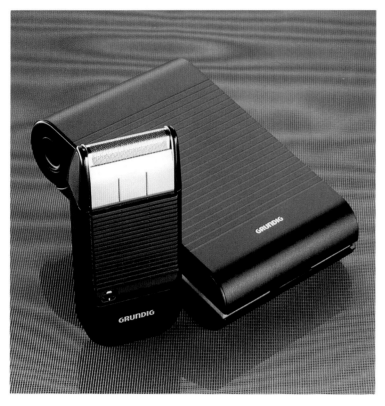

PRODUCT
Roltronic Shaver
DESIGNER
Hans Meelen
FIRM
Philips Corporate Industrial Design
MANUFACTURER
Grundig (Germany); Schick (U.S.A.)

PRODUCT
Beard Trimmer
FIRM
Philips Corporate Industrial Design
AWARD
1987 Gute Industrieform Award,
Germany

PRODUCT
Eltron Mini Battery Shaver
FIRM
Payer, Austria
CLIENT
Becker, Inc.

PRODUCT
Quadron ''CD'' Cord/Cordless
Shaver (#480-42)
FIRM
Robert Krups Stiftung & Co. KG
MANUFACTURER
Matsushita, Japan

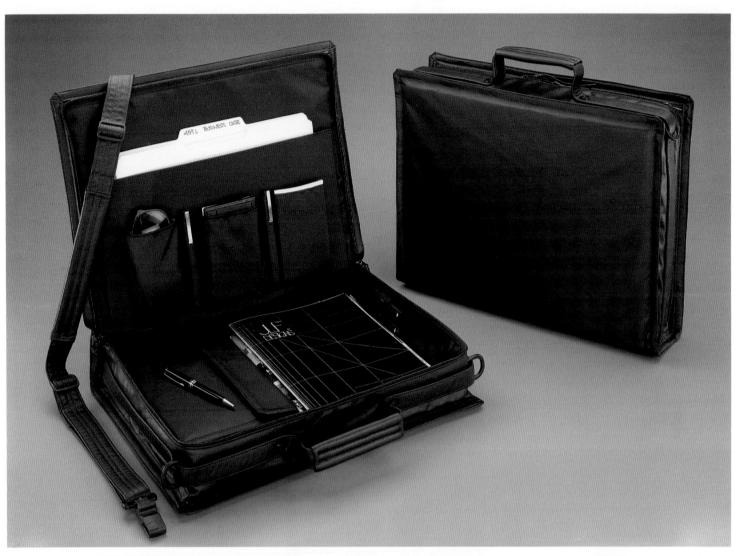

PRODUCT
Business Case
DESIGNER
James L. Fournier
FIRM
JLF Designs
MANUFACTURER
Bennington Leather, Inc.
AWARD
Accent On Design Award, 1987 ID
Design Review

PRODUCT
Samsonite Oyster Luggage
MANUFACTURER
Samsonite, Belgium
CLIENT
Samsonite
AWARD
1988 ID Design Review

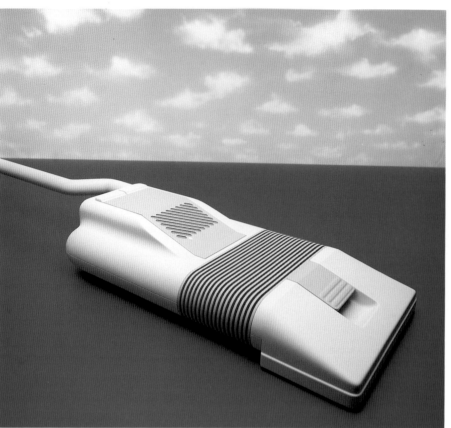

PRODUCT
Vacuum Cleaner
DESIGNER
Vlad Muller
FIRM
Muller/Ullman Industial Designers,
Canada
CLIENT
Muller/Ullmann Industrial Designers

PRODUCT
Compact Vacuum Cleaner
FIRM
Philips Corporate Industrial Design

PRODUCT
Stick Type Vacuum Cleaner
DESIGNER
Design Department Home Appliance
Sector
FIRM
Matsushita Electric Industrial Co.,
Ltd., Japan
MANUFACTURER
Matsushita Electric Industrial Co.,
Ltd.
AWARD
1987 ID Design Review

PRODUCT
Aerospace Luggage
DESIGNER
Douglas Paige
FIRM
Ron Loosen Associates
MANUFACTURER
Andiamo
CLIENT
Andiamo

PRODUCT
Weathervane #121
DESIGNER
Jonathan Bonner

PRODUCT
Garment Bag
DESIGNER
Jeff Bertelsen
FIRM
Tumi Luggage
MANUFACTURER
Tumi Luggage
CLIENT
Tumi Luggage

CHAPTER 9

Gianfranco Zaccai
IDSA, Principle
Design Continuum Inc.

When you see a medical product being used by physicians or nurses, you get a sense of what role it plays in their lives. You also understand that sometimes it's not the focal point of their lives, but really just a tool of their trade. And if that tool gets in their way, it's not used or respected. It's destroyed, lost or broken.

The challenge of design is not simply an aesthetic one. It is instead trying to make something that will be pleasing to all the senses—the visual, the tactile and the sense of propriety—that are appropriate to the doctor in order for him to get his job done.

Design isn't only a question of balancing ergonomic, functional, technical, emotional or aesthetic elements. It's a question of highlighting all those aspects. And in medicine, products must also make sense in terms of mechanical and electronic function, size, weight and convenience. Often these things get redesigned by the user. Sometimes you wander through a lab and see some elegant piece of pristine equipment with flower decals stuck on it, and that's one person's way of saying he or she wants a little more humanity and warmth in front of him. There is an emotional need that needs to be filled.

Medical equipment must provide elements that give prestige to the user, but not at the expense of function, accessibility, maintenance and cleanliness. Now, add to that another factor that is dramatically changing medical design: fear of contagion. With diseases like AIDS and hepatitis, people are handling specimens that are contaminated and there is a real safety concern. It means that we've got to focus very closely on the user and what he does before he even gets to the machine you've designed.

•

I find that sophisticated technology is actually easier to understand and decipher than the human elements. It's really more difficult to understand how people interact with a product than how the components interact with each other. In terms of mechanics, and fluidics and electronics, designers are still using the same physical principles. A lot of our job is to cut through that massive technology and to see the harmony underneath the clutter.

•

Today, with so many specialists to engineer every technically complex field, you need someone to orchestrate them all to make the end result simple, straightforward and accessible. The best person to do that is the designer. Only a small portion of our job happens on paper and in models because sketches and models are only tools. Design is really an artistic and intellectual process and what you're really selling is your vision. You can't capture vision in a superficial drawing or a model. To have a wonderful design, you have to take it further—by looking for ways of integrating and simplifying.

I get inspiration from what happens in the broad spectrum of culture. I take visual inspiration from crafts people and artists, and technical inspiration from materials and processes. It's also important to have a knowledge of history because there is value in what has been done in the past. When you look back you see how cultural forces have been as responsible for design or architecture as designers or architects. And there is also a tremendous value to knowing that you belong to a part of a continuing process.

When Mario Bellini, for example, talks about the wedge shape he used for the Olivetti typewriter, he says he was inspired by a Renaissance writing desk. Whether it was conscious or not, I think there are some forms like a lectern or portable writing desk that lend a symbolic meaning to something like a typewriter.

My own influences come from all over and I can't cite one simple point of reference. If I could, there would be no art, no mystery in design because it would simply be the application of stylistic gimmicks. When I design, I try to find truth and beauty for this particular time in history, in this particular culture.

The function of a pacemaker is to sit in the chest cavity and keep someone's heart beating regularly. All the components should also fit the smallest possible configuration. But there is another level of form, and that is that the object should be beautiful, even if no one sees it. It's similar to the gargoyles on Gothic cathedrals, which were sculpted on all sides even though no one ever saw them from above —except God. Designers should have a similar value system that says that things should be done beautifully for their own sake.

•

I think that all designers should travel and spend significant amounts of time in other cultures. When they spot something that is quite different —not only objects, but ways of doing things—they should question why that is so. Because it is only then that you realize that things could easily be done in other ways. It makes you question, and those questions somehow percolate down to visual design.

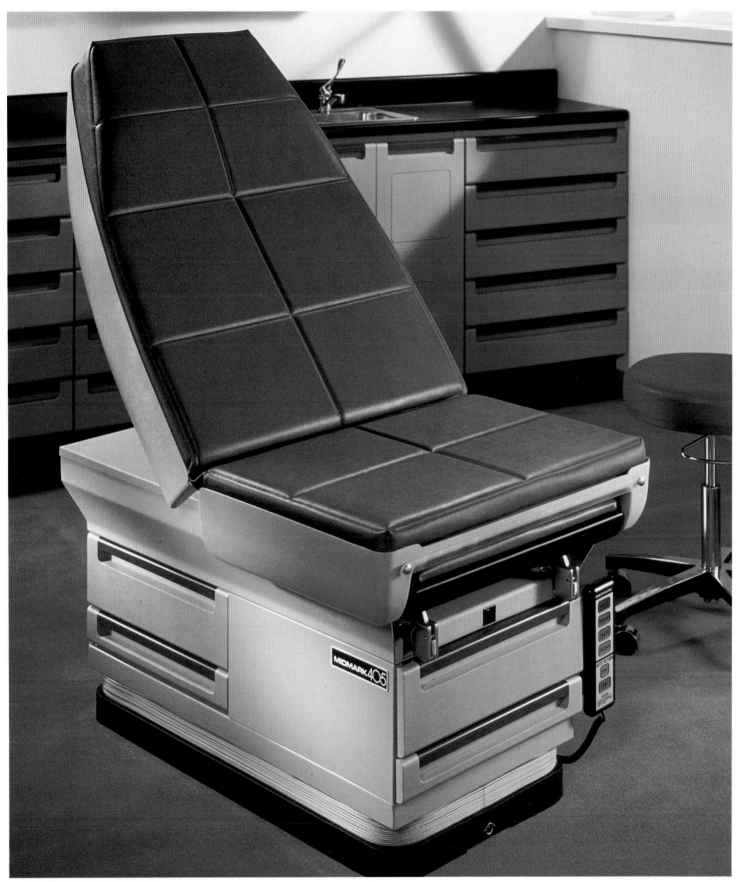

PRODUCT
Midmark 405 Power Exam Table
DESIGNER
Terry J. Simpkins
FIRM
Simpkins Design Group,
Incorporated
MANUFACTURER
Midmark Corporation
CLIENT
Midmark Corporation

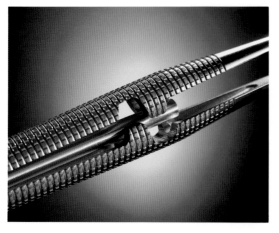

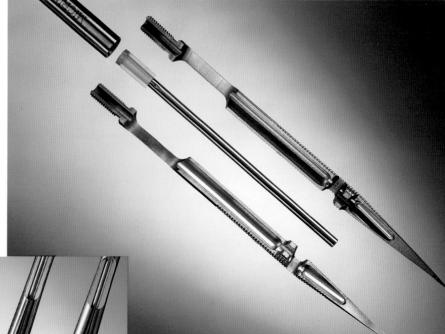

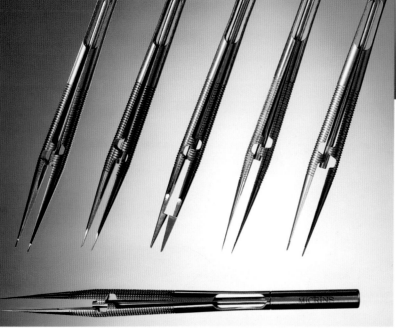

PRODUCT
Micrins Microsurgical Instrument
DESIGNER
Paul Specht
FIRM
Goldsmith Yamasaki Specht Inc.
MANUFACTURER
Micrins
AWARD
1988 ID Design Review Selection

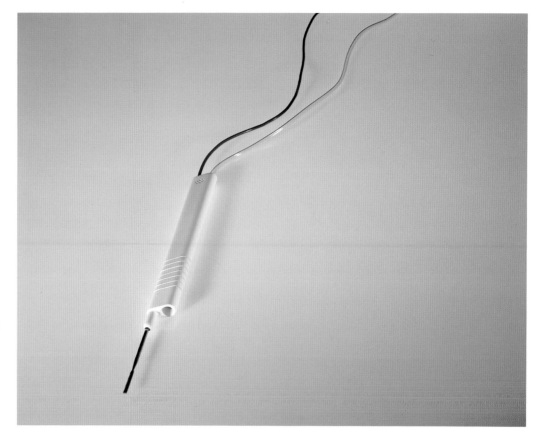

PRODUCT
Electronic Smokeless Scalpel
DESIGNER
Jeff Smith
FIRM
Lunar Design Incorporated
MANUFACTURER
MD Engineering
CLIENT
MD Engineering

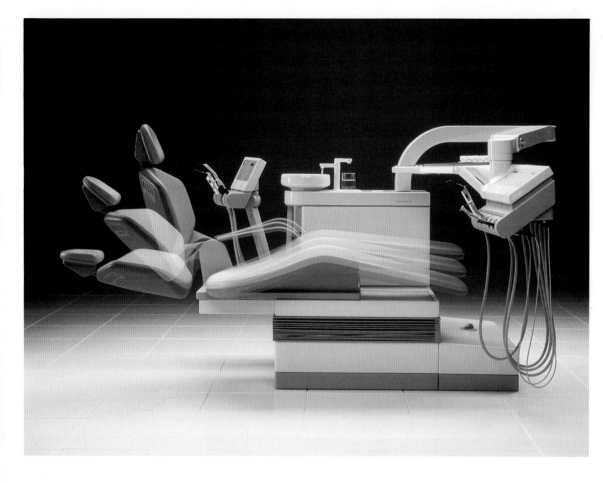

PRODUCT:
KaVo Estetica 1042, Dental Unit
DESIGNER:
Hartmut Esslinger
FIRM:
frogdesign
AWARDS:
Design Center, Stuttgart; ''IF''
Hannover

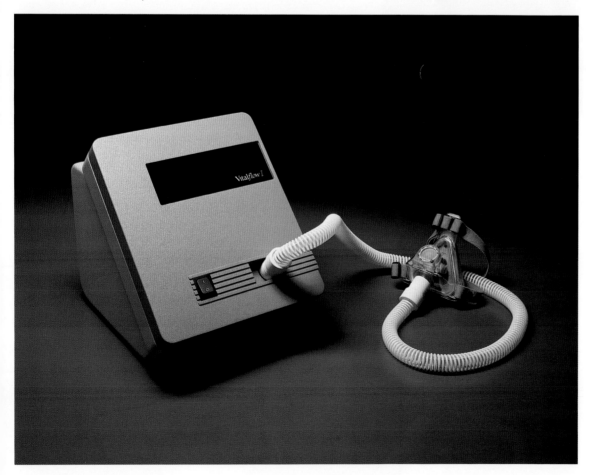

PRODUCT:
VITALFLOW-Nasal CPAP System
DESIGNER:
Juleen Gottesman Mitchell
MANUFACTURER:
Systems 2000, Inc.
CLIENT:
Systems 2000, Inc.
DESCRIPTION:
Delivers airway pressure to patients
whose respiration stops while
sleeping.

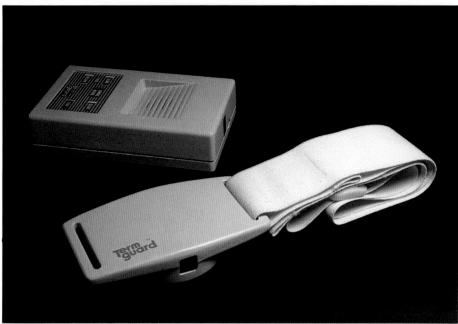

PRODUCT
Term Guard
DESIGNERS
Ravi Sawhney, James Hirsch, Cary
Severn, Ichero Iwaski
FIRM
RKS Design Associates
MANUFACTURER
Tokos Medical Corporation
CLIENT
Barry Hudson And Gary Kinipis
DESCRIPTION
Monitors pregnant patients with
histories of premature deliveries.

PRODUCT
Compuchart Medical Recordkeeping
Terminal
DESIGNER
Ron Boeder
FIRM
Boeder Design
MANUFACTURER
Compuchart
AWARDS
1987 IDEA Award, 1988 Industrial
Design Excellence Award
DESCRIPTION
Portable computer terminal for
storing patient information.

PRODUCT
Medical Air Filter
DESIGNERS
Edgar Montague, Eddie Machen,
James Machen, Tracy Teague
FIRM
Machen Montague, Inc.
MANUFACTURER
Fluid Energy Products
CLIENT
Fluid Energy Products
DESCRIPTION
Disposable unit to filter bacteria and
viruses from air.

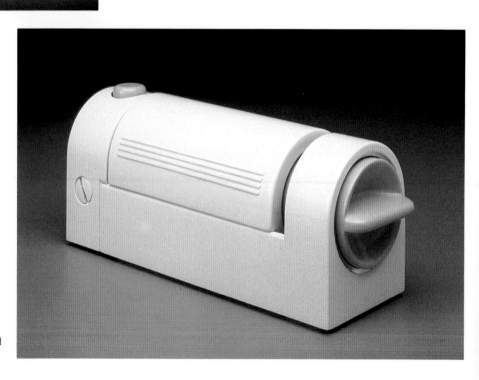

PRODUCT
Critical Care Data Manager
DESIGNERS
LeRoy J. LaCelle, Tony Grasso, and
David Litrell
FIRM
Designhaus, Inc.
CLIENT
Metra
DESCRIPTION
Provides immediate access to all
patient medical records.

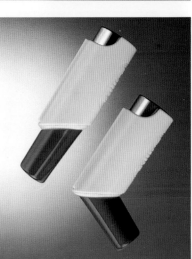

PRODUCT
Asthma Reliever Inhaler
DESIGNER
Barrie Weaver
FIRM
Roberts Weaver Design Limited, UK
MANUFACTURER
Pfizer Pharmaceuticals
CLIENT
Pfizer Pharmaceuticals
DESCRIPTION
Rotating head allows inhaler to be
carried unobtrusively when not in
use.

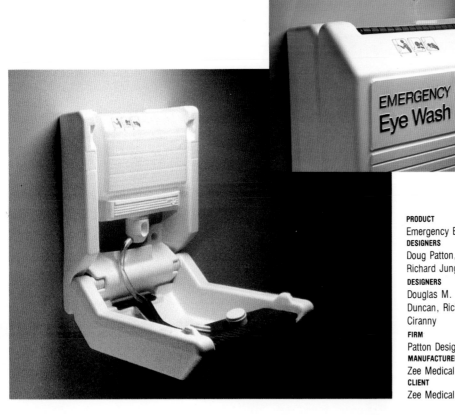

PRODUCT
Emergency Eyewash Station
DESIGNERS
Doug Patton, Matthew Dunc
Richard Jung, Joan Ciranny
DESIGNERS
Douglas M. Patton, Matthew
Duncan, Richard Jung, Joan
Ciranny
FIRM
Patton Design Enterprises
MANUFACTURER
Zee Medical
CLIENT
Zee Medical

PRODUCT
Optacon II
FIRM
Canon Inc., Tokyo
MANUFACTURER
Telesensory Systems, Inc.
CLIENT
Telesensory Systems, Inc.
DESCRIPTION:
Enables blind people to read print or computer screens by converting characters to vibrating tactile form.

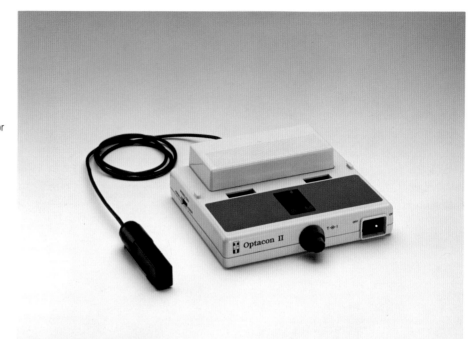

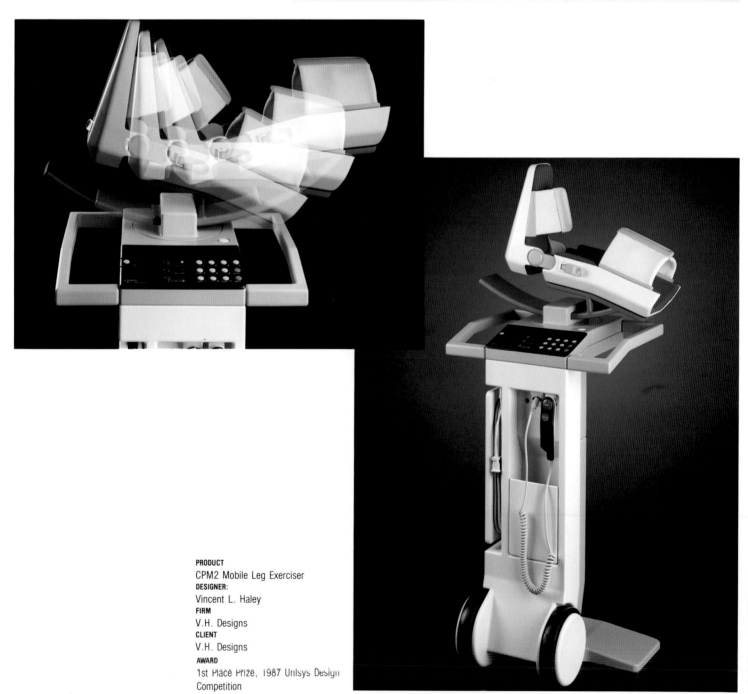

PRODUCT
CPM2 Mobile Leg Exerciser
DESIGNER:
Vincent L. Haley
FIRM
V.H. Designs
CLIENT
V.H. Designs
AWARD
1st Place Prize, 1987 Unisys Design Competition

PRODUCT
Diabetic Management System
(Romeo and Juliet)
FIRM
ninaber/peters/krouwel
MANUFACTURER
Diva Medical Systems, The
Netherlands
CLIENT
Diva Medical Systems
AWARD
1987 Holland In Vorm

PRODUCT
(Maddak) Right Angled Spoon
DESIGNER
James M. Howard
FIRM
Howard Industrial Design Assoc.,
Inc.
MANUFACTURER
Maddak, Inc.
CLIENT
Maddak, Inc.
DESCRIPTION
Facilitates self-feeding for the
handicapped

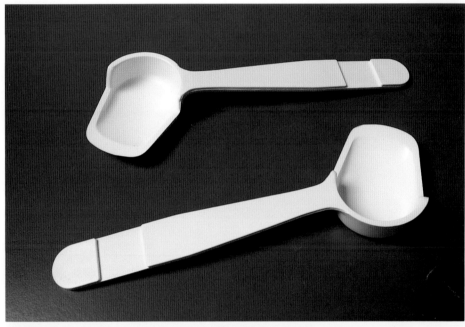

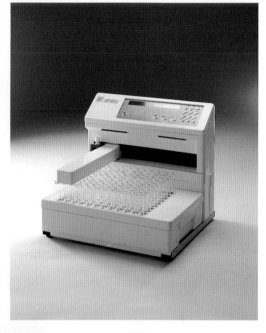

PRODUCT
Fraction Collector
DESIGNER
Touru Hanada
FIRM
Hirano & Associates, Inc.
MANUFACTURER
Avantec Toyo Chemical Industry
Co., Ltd., Japan
CLIENT
Advantec Toyo Chemical Industry
Co., Ltd.

PRODUCT
Malaria Microscope and Centrifuge
DESIGNERS
Stephen G. Hauser—Industrial
Designer, Manny Fernandez—
Mechanical Engineer, James Karney
—Optical Engineer, Dave Weinkle—
Electrical Engineer
MANUFACTURER
Becton Dickinson and Company
CLIENT
Becton Dickinson and Company
DESCRIPTION
Battery powered fluoresence
microscope designed to identify
malaria in blood samples.

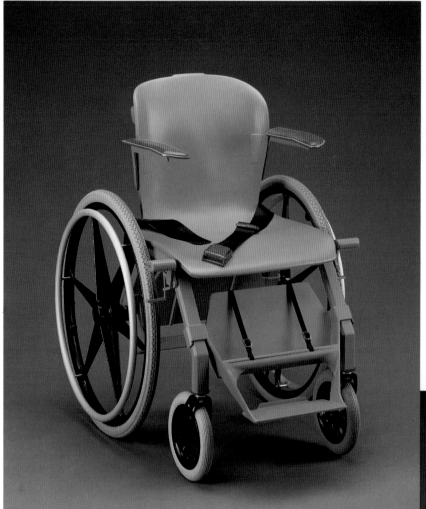

PRODUCT
The Lindde Wheel Chair—
Conceptual
DESIGNER
Linda Petchnick
FIRM
Lin Design
AWARD
1988 Northwest Design Invitational
Honorable Mention

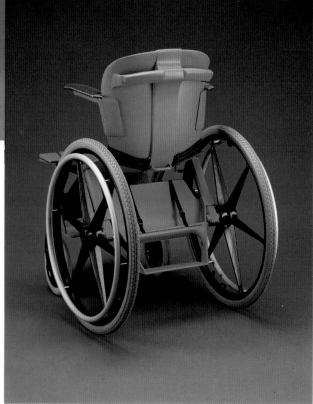

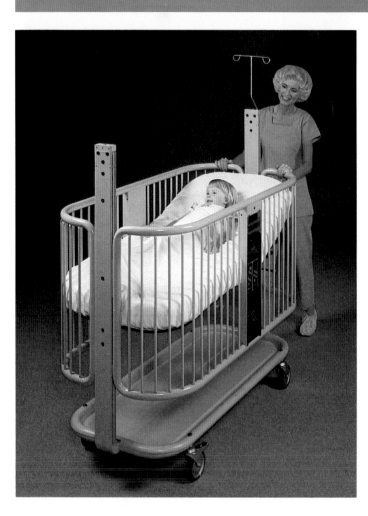

PRODUCT
Model 500 Stretcher/Crib (Pediatric)
DESIGNERS
Terry J. Simpkins, David Harris
FIRM
Simpkins Design Group,
Incorporated
MANUFACTURER
Midmark Corporation
CLIENT
Midmark Corporation
AWARD
1986 ID Design Review

PRODUCT
''Impulse'' Racing Wheelchair
DESIGNER
Lee R. Thorn
MANUFACTURER
Everest & Jennings

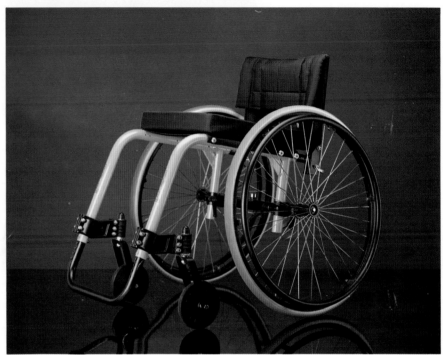

PRODUCT
Champion 3000
DESIGNER
Rainer Kuschall
FIRM
Paratec AG Ltd., Switzerland
MANUFACTURER:
Kuschall of America
CLIENT
Kuschall of America

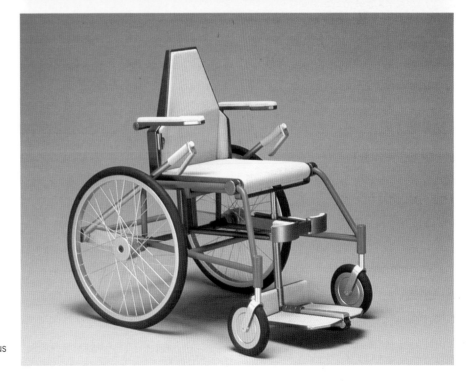

PRODUCT
Sit-Up/Stand-Up Wheelchair
DESIGNER
Andreas Bergstrasser
FIRM
Braun, W. Germany
AWARD
1986 Braun Prize
DESCRIPTION
Permits paralytics to take various
positions.

Khodi Feiz
ISDA
Industrial Designer
Texas Instruments

When I think of design history, I don't think of Dreyfuss or Lowey as the founders. I think of the Stone Age when people had to make tools out of stone, because to me, design is a thought pattern expressed. It's creation, not copying. Good design is inherently simple, pure, and free of pretension. It has survived the process of experimentation and evolution.

The igloo and the tepee are good examples. The igloo provides comfortable shelter in sub-zero temperatures even though it is made of ice (not an automatic choice of materials when you think of protection and warmth). Its form—the dome—is efficient in structure and appropriate to its materials. The tepee is also true to its purpose: it is light and transportable. The conical shape is beautiful and simple, in harmony with the nature it occupies.

•

I started the scuba helmet (page 240) as my thesis project at Syracuse University because it seemed that the scuba industry was lagging behind in design and technical innovation. It's always been a technological sport but it hasn't made the same jump that skiing has, for example. I never scuba dove so I took a class at Syracuse and I met a professional commercial diver whose job was to go underwater to work on pipes. I borrowed ideas from him because it seems that commercial diving seemed like it has better developed techniques.

I came in very naively, with an almost blank mind, and I managed to come up with new ideas. Now that I can dive, I look back and think I wouldn't have approached it the same way. And I probably wouldn't have had the same results. By asking questions, you learn so much.

I also design products for kids, and when I asked them why they didn't like educational toys, I learned that they thought they were boring. From that I tried to find out what they *do* like, so I could translate it into products that they would enjoy playing with and could learn from at the

same time. It's the user-oriented approach that I like. Rather than form following function, I think it's more like form follows the function of the person using it.

•

Designing new sports equipment or a workout program should be treated like any other design problem: the goal should be to create a product that is simpler, more accessible, more comfortable and safe; to create an object or an environment that is appealing and approachable, not cold or intimidating.

In his books, *The Timeless Way of Building* and *Pattern Language,* Christopher Alexander touches upon the notion of products speaking to consumers. He calls it "the quality without a name." When this quality exists, certain products seem to have lives unto themselves. They are not arbitrary and dead. They have been created with a purpose and a function, and the care in their creation gives them a specialness which is not evident in lesser products. They have a calm, comfortable feeling that only comes when you as a designer are true to your purpose and work.

•

We redesign a teapot or a computer over and over again for completely different reasons. A non-technical object like a teapot has gone through its evolutionary phase and now can simply exist as an "object." The process of creation is free and there is room for statements. This redefinition of objects like teapots and chairs will always continue, and subtle nuances that were previously not seen will be introduced.

The technical object is another story. The computer has not reached its evolutionary end. It is still changing technically and in order to cater to these changes, it will be systematically redesigned. Not until that technical process has peaked will we have explorations of that object for its own sake.

•

It is very difficult to pinpoint a specific design signature for the '80s. The times have become

more complex and less focused and therefore, harder to pin down. I think that the acceptance of new ideas and camps of thought, and the freedom to break away from doctrine, is a sign of maturation for design. You can see one example of this freedom in the work from the Memphis group. Even though others were doing similar work in the '70s, it was Memphis that opened our eyes. Another area for the '80s is "global design" and worldwide marketing; we see many consultant firms and corporate design centers focusing on international growth.

In the '90s, I hope we can shift gears and contribute socially and environmentally to the world's problems. As designers, we have knowledge and skills that are not available, say, in the Third World. We need to give people there our knowledge, not just our products; we need to show them that they can work with certain materials, as opposed to just going in and making them reliant on us. Socially responsible design, I hope, will be the signature not only of the '90s, but the established doctrine for the future.

PRODUCT
CCM Stationary Bicycle
DESIGNER
Michel Dallaire
FIRM
Michel Dallaire Designers, Inc.
MANUFACTURER
PRO-FIT Exercisers Canada Inc.
CLIENT
Procycle Ltd.

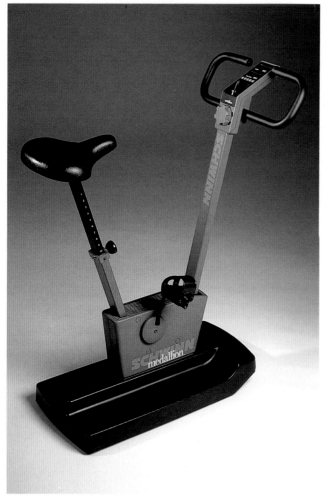

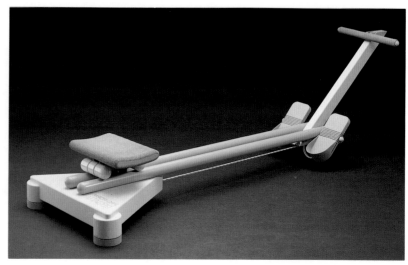

PRODUCT
Regatta
DESIGNERS
Sohab Vossoughi, Bill Daleabout,
Nancy Dalton
FIRM
Ziba Design
MANUFACTURER
Weslo, Inc.
CLIENT
Pro-Form, Inc.
AWARD
1988 IDSA Northwest Design
Invitational

PRODUCT
Cycle Exerciser Schwinn Medallion
DESIGNERS
Marlan Polhemus, Lakshmi
Narayan-Burns
FIRM
Goldsmith Yamasaki Specht, Inc.
MANUFACTURER
Schwinn Bicycle Company
CLIENT
Schwinn Bicycle Company

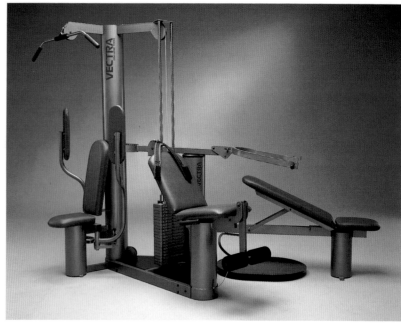

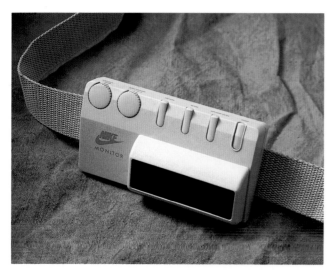

PRODUCT
Nike Monitor 1000
DESIGNERS
Sohrab Vossoughi, Bill Daleabout
FIRM
Ziba Design
MANUFACTURER
Nike, Inc.
CLIENT
Nike, Inc.
DESCRIPTION
Electronic audio feedback device for
monitoring speed, pace, distance or
pulse during exercise.

PRODUCT:
Vectra Fitness On-Line 1500
DESIGNERS:
Loyd Moore, Steve Kaneko –
Technology Design
Buel Ish, Jeffrey Johnson – Vectra
Fitness
MANUFACTURER:
Vectra Fitness
CLIENT:
Vectra Fitness

PRODUCT
Mirrcycle Bicycle Mirror
DESIGNER
Barry Schacht
MANUFACTURER
Mirrcycle Corp.

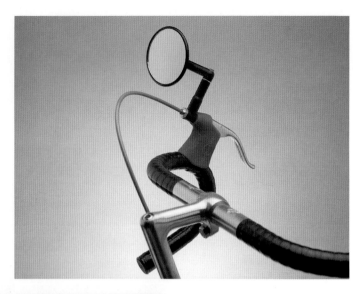

PRODUCT
Bicycle PFT-7000
DESIGNER
Matsushita Electric Industrial Co.,
Ltd., Bicycle Division, Japan
FIRM
Matsushita Electric Industrial Co.,
Ltd.

PRODUCT
Beveltech Bicycle
DESIGNER
Product Planning Department
FIRM
GK Inc., Japan
MANUFACTURER
Maruishi Cycling Industries, Ltd.
CLIENT
Maruishi Cycling Industries, Ltd.

PRODUCT:
''Blouson'' Unisex Bicycle
FIRM:
Giugiaro Design, Italy
MANUFACTURER:
Bridgstone

PRODUCT:
Folding Bike
DESIGNER:
Ng Yim Kwong

PRODUCT:
Folding Bike
DESIGNER:
Ng Yim Kwong, Hong Kong
AWARD:
Hong Kong International Youth
Festival Prize

PRODUCT
Via Pushchair
DESIGNER
Conran Design Group Products
Team
FIRM
Conran Design Group, UK
MANUFACTURER
Britax Restmor, Bissell Appliances
(mouldings)
CLIENT
Mothercare UK
AWARD
1987 Horners Award For
Imaginative Use Of Plastic

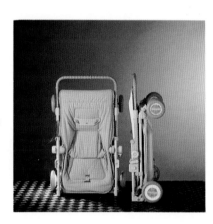

PRODUCT
Hillcrest Golf Motorcaddie
DESIGNERS
Edgar Montague, Eddie Machen,
James Machen
FIRM
Machen Montague
MANUFACTURER
Kangaroo Products Company
CLIENT
Kangaroo Products Company
AWARD
1988 ID Design Review Selection

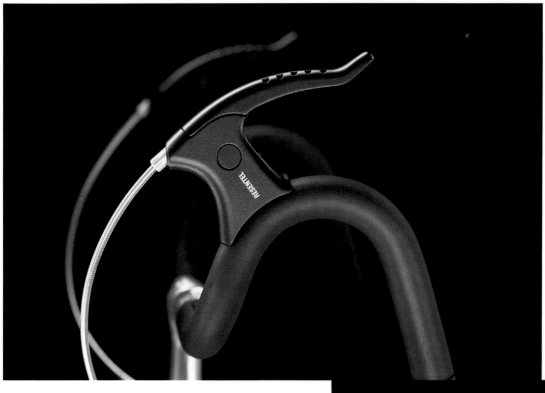

PRODUCT:
Resentel Bicycle Hand Brakes
DESIGNER:
Michel Dallaire
FIRM:
Michel Dallaire Designers Inc.,
Canada
MANUFACTURER:
La Compagnie Resentel Ltee
CLIENT:
La Compagnie Ltee
AWARD:
1986 Canada ''Gold Award'' For
Design Excellence

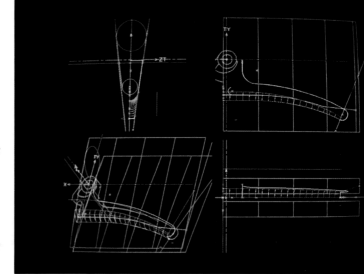

PRODUCT
''AXIOM'' Advanced High
Performance Motorcycle
DESIGNER
Douglas Barber
FIRM
Douglas Barber Design
AWARD
Giugetto Giugaro Award For
Creativity

PRODUCT
Harris 180 Deckboat
DESIGNERS
Terry J. Simpkins,
T.J. Simpkins, Jr.
FIRM
Simpkins Design Group,
Incorporated
MANUFACTURER
Harris-Kayot, Inc.
CLIENT
Harris-Kayot, Inc.

PRODUCT
Motorcycle FZR 1000 (1000cc)
DESIGNER
Dynamic Design Division
FIRM
GK Industrial Design Associates
Tokyo
MANUFACTURER
Yamaha Motor Co., Ltd.
CLIENT
Yamaha Motor Co., Ltd.

PRODUCT
''Cruise'' Prototype Car
DESIGNER
Transportation Design Department
FIRM
GK Industrial Design Associates,
Tokyo
MANUFACTURER
Transportation Design Department
CLIENT
Autorama Inc.

PRODUCT
Navagraphic LORAN Track Plotter
DESIGNERS
Daniele De Iulis, Nick Dormon,
Bruce Browne
FIRM
ID TWO
CLIENT
Trimble Navigation
AWARD
1988 D&AD British Product Design
Award

PRODUCT
Yachting Console
DESIGNERS
Spencer Murrell, Ken Brazell
FIRM
RichardsonSmith, Inc.
MANUFACTURER
Trojan Yachts
CLIENT
Trojan Yachts

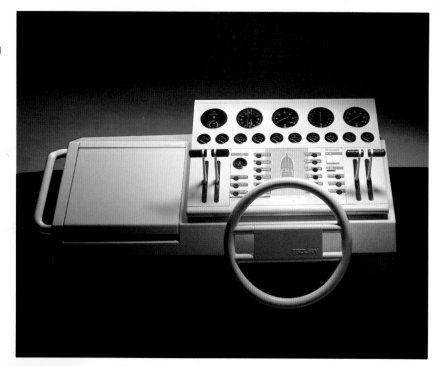

PRODUCT
Navigational Marine Lights
DESIGNER
Barrie Weaver
FIRM
Roberts Weaver Design Ltd., UK
MANUFACTURER
Lucas Marine
CLIENT
Lucas Marine

PRODUCT
820 Series Baitcasting Reel
DESIGNER
John H. Betts
FIRM
Henry Dreyfuss Associates
MANUFACTURER
Abu Garcia Produktion AB
CLIENT
Abu Garcia Produktion AB

PRODUCT
1020 Series Baitcasting Reel
DESIGNER
John H. Betts
FIRM
Henry Dreyfuss Associates
MANUFACTURER
Abu Garcia Produktion AB
CLIENT
Abu Garcia Produktion AB
AWARD
1987 ID Design Review Selection

PRODUCT
MGC–35
FIRM
Mizuno Golf Co.
MANUFACTURER
Mizuno Golf Co.
DESCRIPTION
35% larger than conventional clubs
for greater striking areas.

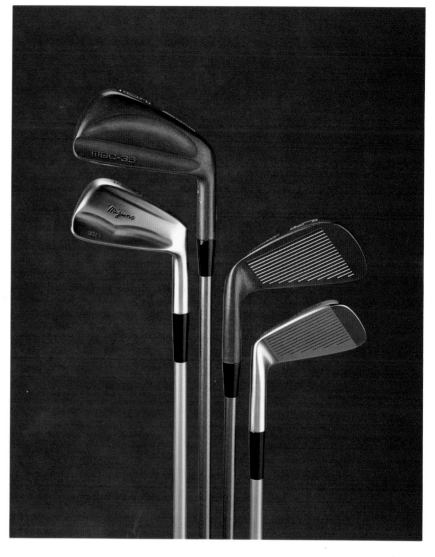

PRODUCT
"Swivel" Adjustable Putter
DESIGNER
Aldo Balatti
CLIENT
Innovative Products International,
Canada
AWARD
1987 ID Design Review Honorable
Mention

PRODUCT
Response ZT Putter
DESIGNER
D. Clayton Long
FIRM
MacGregor Golf Company
MANUFACTURER
MacGregor Golf Company

PRODUCT
''Edge'' Snowboard
DESIGNER
Bob Katz
FIRM
Katz Design Inc., Canada
MANUFACTURER
SLM Action Sports Inc.
CLIENT
SLM Action Sports Inc.

PRODUCT
SLM Golf Cart
DESIGNER
Michel Dallaire
FIRM
Michel Dallaire Designers Inc.
MANUFACTURER
SLM (Saint-Laurence Manufacturing
Canada Inc.)
CLIENT
SLM

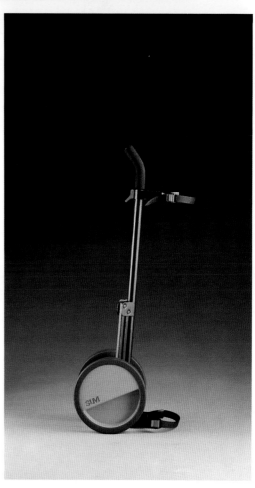

PRODUCT
Huski Ski Valet
DESIGNERS
Peter W. Bressler, Peter D. Byar,
Ben BEck, P. Ken Rossi
FIRM
Bresslergroup
MANUFACTURER
Magwin Enterprises
CLIENT
Magwin Enterprises

PRODUCT
Raichle RX 979
DESIGNER
Research And Development Team
FIRM
Raichle Sportschuh AG
MANUFACTURER
Raichle Sportschuh, Switzerland
DESCRIPTION
''Flow substance'' allows inner boot
to mold to each wearer's foot.

PRODUCT
''SNOSCOOT'' Snow Vehicle
DESIGNER
Dynamic Design Division
FIRM
GK Industrial Design Associates
MANUFACTURER:
Yamaha Motor Co., Ltd.
CLIENT
Yamaha Motor Co., Ltd.
FIRM
GK Industrial Design Associates,
Japan

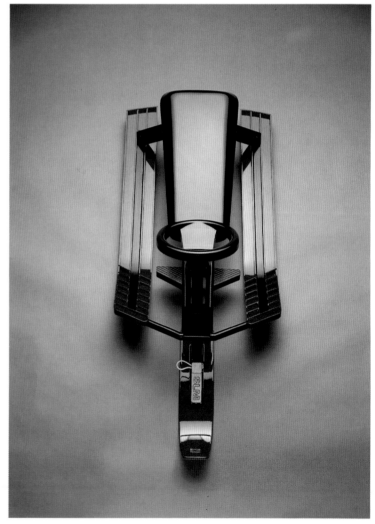

PRODUCT
Snofox Tri-Ski
DESIGNER
Michel Dallaire
FIRM
Michel Dallaire Designers Inc.
MANUFACTURER
SLM (Saint-Laurence Manufacturing
Canada Inc.)
CLIENT
SLM Inc.

PRODUCT
Nava Skiing System
DESIGNER
Pier Luigi
FIRM
Nava Leisure
MANUFACTURER
Nava Moto S.p.A., Italy
DESCRIPTION
Sift ski boot with binding that
allows multi-directional release.

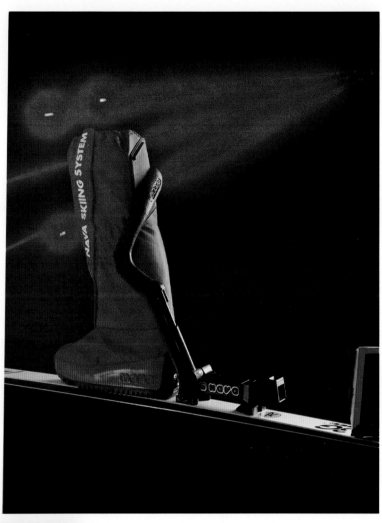

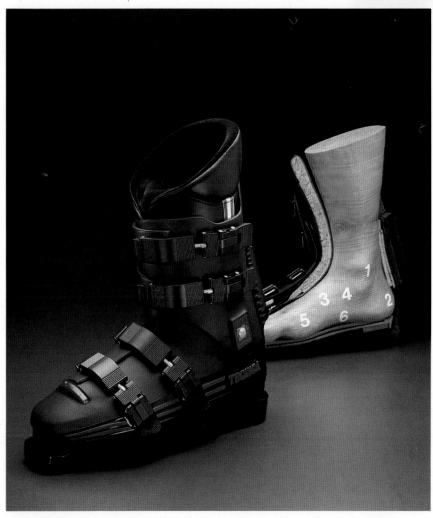

PRODUCT
Ski Boot
DESIGNERS
Antonello Marega (SPA), Peter
Knights (U.S.A.)
FIRM.
Tecnica SPA, Italy, Tecnica U.S.A.
MANUFACTURER
Tecnica

PRODUCT
Spectra Fins/Mask/Snorkel
DESIGNER
Ralph Osterhout
FIRM
Tekna
MANUFACTURER
Tekna

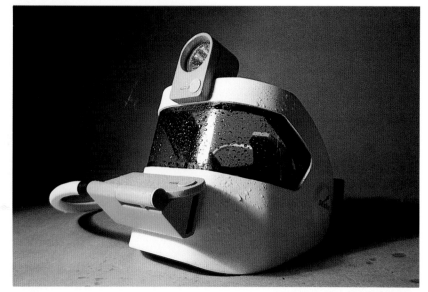

PRODUCT
Intergrated Scuba Helmut
DESIGNER
Khodi Feiz (student project)
AWARD
1987 International Design
Competition, Osaka
DESCRIPTION
Underwater unit incorporating mask,
regulator, gauges and underwater
communication.

PRODUCT:
''Aquatch'' Sport Dive Watch
DESIGNERS:
Michael Karff, Drew Collot
MANUFACTURER:
Freestyle U.S.A.
PHOTO:
Jack A. Thistle
DESCRIPTION:
Surfing watch containing canisters
for skin lotion.

PRODUCT
Tyco Turbo Train
DESIGNERS
Joel Carpenter and
Tyco Design Staff
FIRM
The Design Works
MANUFACTURER
Tyco Industries, Inc.
CLIENT
Tyco Industries, Inc.
DESCRIPTION
The world's fastest toy train.

PRODUCT
Children's Outdoor Play Equipment
DESIGNER
Jenifer King
FIRM
Northwest Design Products, Inc.
MANUFACTURER
BigToys

PRODUCT
Blue-Fox Electric Car
DESIGNER
Quod
FIRM
Quod Disseny i Marketing, S.A.,
Spain
MANUFACTURER
Feber, S.A.
CLIENT
Jugetes Feber, S.A.
DESCRIPTION
A cross between an all terrain
vehicle and formula one racer for 5
to 10 year olds.

PRODUCT
The Ultimate Instant Replay Device
DESIGNERS
Robert Brunner, Ken Wood
FIRM
Lunar Design Inc.
CLIENT
ID Magazine Fantasy Portfolio

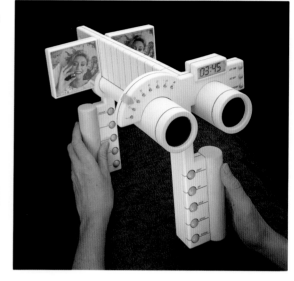

PRODUCT
Arcobaleno
DESIGNERS
Karen Hewitt, Michael Delaney
FIRM
Learning Materials Workshop
AWARD
1986 Parent's Choice Award

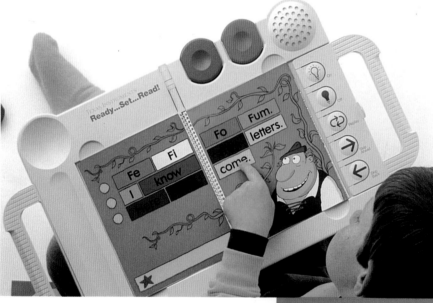

PRODUCT
"Ready...Set...Read!"
DESIGNER
Khodi Feiz
FIRM
Texas Instruments
MANUFACTURER
Texas Instruments
CLIENT
Texas Instruments

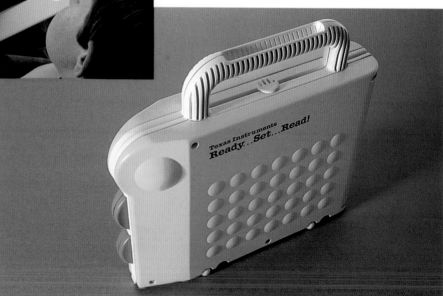

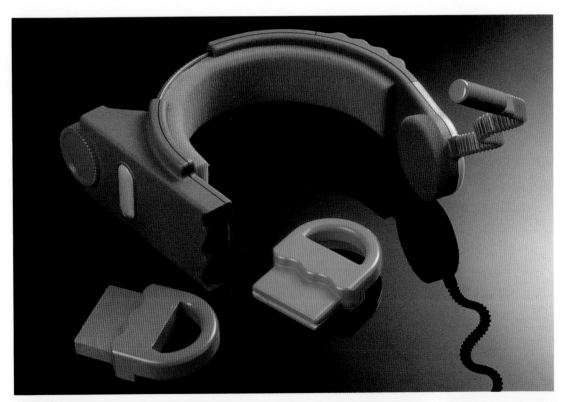

PRODUCT
Texas Instruments Voyager
DESIGNERS
James Couch, Elizabeth B.-N. Sanders, Keith Kresge
FIRM
RichardsonSmith, Inc.
MANUFACTURER
Texas Instruments
CLIENT
Texas Instruments
AWARDS
1988 ID Design Review Selection; 1988 IDEA Design Excellence Award
DESCRIPTION
Using voice-interactive technology, Voyager offers computer generated questions which children answer; a post modern twenty questions.

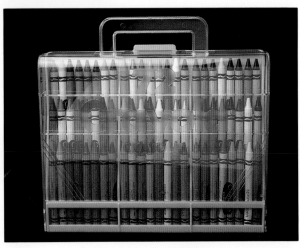

PRODUCT
Crayola Crayon Mega-set Case
DESIGNERS
Davin Stowell, Tom Dair
FIRM
Smart Design
CLIENT
Binney and Smith/Crayola

PRODUCT
Popsickle Trays
DESIGNERS
Brent Markee, Tom Dair
FIRM
Smark Design
MANUFACTURER
Eagle Affiliates
CLIENT
Eagle Affiliates

PRODUCT
Project n Sketch
DESIGNERS
D.M. Gresham, Martin Thaler,
James Ludwig
FIRM
Design Logic
MANUFACTURER
View-Master Ideal Group

PRODUCT
Teddy Ruxpin
DESIGNERS
Ravi Sawhney, James Middleton
FIRM
RKS Design Associates
MANUFACTURER
Worlds Of Wonder
CLIENT
Alchemy II, Ken Forse

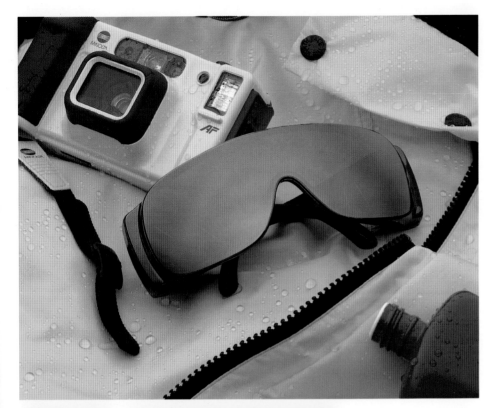

PRODUCT
Zurich III Sunglasses/Ski Goggles
DESIGNER
Bruce Holden
FIRM
Zurich International
MANUFACTURER
Zurich International
CLIENT
Zurich International
PHOTO
Charles Imstepf

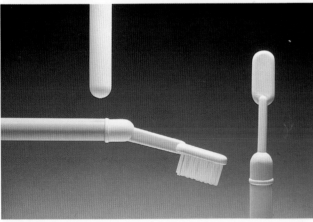

PRODUCT
Toothbrush
DESIGNER
Winfried Scheuer
FIRM
Moggridge Associates, UK
AWARD
1987 Forma Finlandia International
Plastics Design Competition

PRODUCT
Cut Vegetable Toy
DESIGNER:
Hideaki Nakai
FIRM
Moku Co., Ltd., Japan
MANUFACTURER
Moku Co., Ltd.
AWARD
1987 Good Design Prize For Small
Industry Products

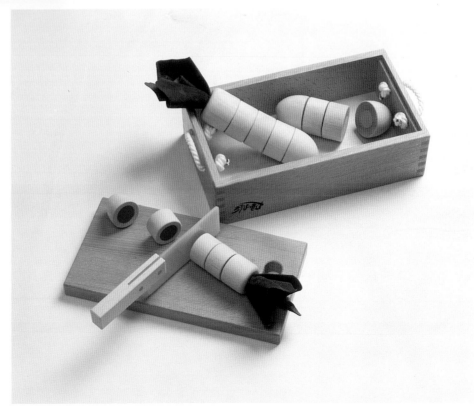

PRODUCT
"Tadpole" Tent
DESIGNER
Doug Brown
FIRM
Doug Brown Associates
MANUFACTURER
The North Face
AWARDS
1987 IDEA Award; BACKPACKER
MAGAZINE Product Design Award

PRODUCT
"Laser Hi-Wall" Lacrosse Stick
With Handle
DESIGNER
STX, Inc.
FIRM
STX, Inc.
MANUFACTURER
STX, Inc.

PRODUCT
Yo
DESIGNER
Earl Gee
FIRM
Mark Anderson Design
MANUFACTURER
One Of A Kind, Ltd.
CLIENT
One Of A Kind, Ltd.

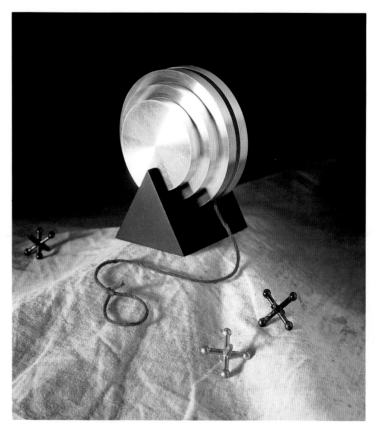

PRODUCT
CXG Superenterprise Chess Playing
Computer
DESIGNER
Geoff Hollington
FIRM
Hollington Associates, UK
MANUFACTURER
White and Alcock
CLIENT
White and Alcock

PRODUCT
Paper Chess
DESIGNER
Peter Hewitt
CLIENT
Museum of Modern Art
PHOTOGRAPHER
Aaron Rezny
PHOTO
Aaron Rezny

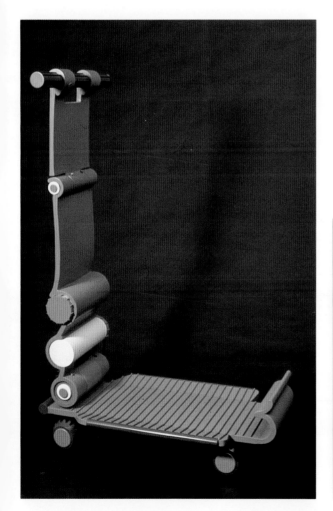

PRODUCT
''Tutti Scutti'' Motorized Skateboard
DESIGNERS
Ellen Cohen, Susanne Pierce
FIRM
Student Project for frogdesign

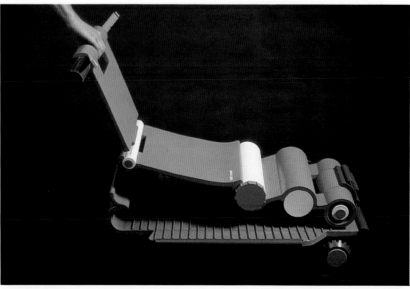

PRODUCT
Adult Finger Paints
DESIGNER
Krista Huebner
FIRM
Fusion Designers & Assoc., Inc.
MANUFACTURER
Cosmoda, Toronto
CLIENT
Fusione

PRODUCT
Puzzle ''Pablo''
DESIGNER
Brent Tervey
MANUFACTURER
Fox Spielverlag GmbH
CLIENT
Davis-Grabowski, Inc.

PRODUCT
frollerskates
DESIGNER
Hartmut Esslinger
FIRM
frogdesign
MANUFACTURER
Indusco
AWARD
1987 Business Week Product Of
The Year

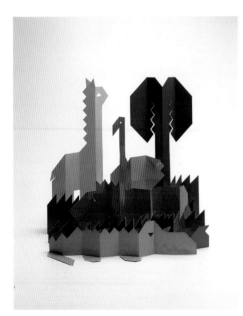

PRODUCT
ARK-I-PETS
DESIGNER
Jack Stone
MANUFACTURER
Paper Sources International, Inc.
CLIENT
Museum of Modern Art
PHOTOGRAPHER
Aaron Rezny

PRODUCT
''Zolo''
DESIGNERS
Byron Glaser, Sandra Higashi
FIRM
Higashi Glaser Design
MANUFACTURER
Higashi Glaser Design
CLIENT
Museum of Modern Art

Index

MANUFACTURERS

CLIENTS

DESIGNERS

DESIGN FIRM ADDRESSES

Ahlstrom-Iittala, Inc. 16, 25
175 Clearbrook Ave., Elmsford, NY 10523

Airon 86
V. dun Sturzo 10, 20050 Triuggio, Milano, ITALY

Alan Tye Design 204
Great West Plantation, Tring, Herts, ENGLAND

Aldo Balatti
5 Massey So.♯♯ 2703, Toronto, Ontario, CANADA M4C 5L6

Alessi 31 202, 203
28023 Crusinallo, (no) Italia

Anderson/Schwartz 169
40 Hudson Street, New York, NY 10012

Andrea Stix Wasserman 116
96 Fort Greene Place, Brooklyn, NY 11217

Andree Putnam
c/o Studio Ecart, 111 Rue Saint Antoine, 75004 Paris, FRANCE

Angela Knoop
Hamburg, WEST GERMANY

Annie Glass Studio 20
303 Potriro Street ♯♯8, Santa Cruz, CA 95060

Apple Computer Incorporated 126, 130, 138   20525 Mariani Ave., M/S 22-L, Cupertino, CA 95014

Archetype Gallery 40 119
411 East 9th Street, New York, NY 10009

Archivo Frau 73
62029 Tolentino, ITALY

AREA Design Inc., Toronto 82
334 King Street East, Toronto, Ontario, CANADA M5A 1K8

Artemide, Inc. 157
1980 New Highway, Farmingdale, NY 11735

Art et Industrie 72, 84, 95, 161, 162   106 Spring Street, New York, NY   10012

Art People 117, 123
594 Broadway, New York, NY 10012

Ashcraft Design 53, 54, 64
11832 W. Pico Blvd., Los Angeles, CA 90064

Associate Designers SA 157
Pl. Gironella, ♯♯1, Barcelona, 80817 SPAIN

Atelier Int'l., Limited 73
30-20 Thomson Avenue, Long Island City, NY 11101

Atlantic Design 49, 199
6 Newburgh Street, London, ENGLAND W1V 1LH

Bawet, SA
C. Arago
333 Baixos 08009
Barcelona, SPAIN

Bartlett Design Assoc., Inc. 143,
614 Santa Barbara Street, Suite D, Santa Barbara, CA 93101

Bernal/Isern 35, 102
Angu N 6 Bajos. 08017 Barcelona, SPAIN

Bharat Electronics Ltd.
11T, Powai, Bombay, INDIA

Black & Decker and Group Four 200
6 Armstrong Road, Shelton, CT 06484

Blast 15, 16
Box 5183, Santa Cruz, CA 95063

Blau Commercial S.A., Spain 98
42-44 Miguel Romeu, 08901 L'Hospitalet, De Llobregat, Barcelona, SPAIN

Boda Nova 38
Kungsgatan 33, Stockholm, SWEDEN

Boeder Design 220
1132 Tulane Ct., Livermore, CA 94550

Braun, West Germany 225
Frankfurterstrasse 15, D-6242 Kronberg iM Taunus, GERMANY 0617330

Bresslergroup 143, 190, 237
301 Cherry Street, Philadelphia, PA 19106

Brezavar & Brezavar, Architects 96
115 West 29th Street, New York, NY 10001

Canetti, Inc. 41, 71, 108, 173, 186
230 Fifth Avenue, New York, NY 10001

Canon Incorporated 69   A...
7-1 Nish. Shintuku, 2 Chrome Shinjuko-ku, Tokyo, 165, JAPAN

Capri Lighting 166
6430 E. Slauson, Los Angeles, CA 90040

Carleton Designs 119
1015A Greenwood Road, Elk, CA 95432

Casaform 72
200 Lexington Avenue, ♯♯ 512, New York, NY 10016

Chan & Dolan Industrial Design Incorporated 59, 137, 168
285 W. Broadway, Suite 650, New York, NY 10013

Charles Rozier Design 50
170 Lafayette Street, New York, NY 10012

Chateau X 118
250 Mener Street, New York, NY 10012

Chris Barlow
20 Pembridge, Nottinghill Gate, W11 42S, London, ENGLAND

Christoph Boeninger
IDSA, VDID
425 Park Avenue South, New York, NY 10016

Clodagh, Incorporated 29
365 First Avenue, New York, NY 10010

Clodagh, Ross & Williams
260 Morris Avenue, Providence, RI 02906

Comspec
Pan Am Bldg., 200 Park Avenue, New York, NY 10166

Conram Design Group, U.K. 231
196 Tottenham Court Rd., London W1P 9LD ENGLAND

Contemporary Porcelain Gallery 23, 35, 44
105 Sullivan Street
New York, NY 10012

Contours Consulting Design Group Inc. 62
864 Stearns Road, Bartlett, IL 60103

Cooper Tools 191, 194
3535 Glenwood Avenue, Raleigh, NC 27612

Creadesign Ky 79
Laivanvarustajankatu 9, 00140 Helsinki, FINLAND

PHOTOGRAPHERS